User-Centered Design

WITHDRAWN

Travis Lowdermilk

O'REILLY®

Beijing · Cambridge · Farnham · Köln · Sebastopol · Tokyo

User-Centered Design

by Travis Lowdermilk

Printed in the United States of America.

Published by O'Reilly Media, Inc., 1005 Gravenstein Highway North, Sebastopol, CA 95472.

O'Reilly books may be purchased for educational, business, or sales promotional use. Online editions are also available for most titles (*http://my.safaribooksonline.com*). For more information, contact our corporate/institutional sales department: 800-998-9938 or *corporate@oreilly.com*.

Editor: Mary Treseler	**Indexer:** Ellen Troutman Zaig
Production Editor: Kara Ebrahim	**Cover Designer:** Randy Comer
Copyeditor: Amanda Kersey	**Interior Designer:** David Futato
Proofreader: Kiel Van Horn	**Illustrator:** Kara Ebrahim

April 2013: First Edition

Revision History for the First Edition:

2013-03-28: First release

See *http://oreilly.com/catalog/errata.csp?isbn=9781449359805* for release details.

ISBN: 978-1-449-35980-5

[LSI]

For my wife—thank you for encouraging me to dream.

For my two boys—thank you for being the reason I still dream.

For my brother—thank you for telling me when it's time to wake up.

Table of Contents

Preface

Is This Book Right for Me?

I sure hope so. Let's see if I can help set expectations.

In the many years I've been building applications, I've spent a great deal of time trying to understand users. I'm obsessed with figuring out how they tick: What motivates them? What frustrates them? What makes them choose one application over another? What can I do to get them to choose *my* applications?

Based on the many discussions I've had with developers from all over the world, it's safe to assume that I'm not alone. So, I've decided to write this book to help developers better understand their users. This book is not meant for the user experience (UX) professional or professional designer. Instead, my goal is to help uninitiated developers understand the fundamental practices of user-centered design, usability, and user experience.

This discussion should be your launch pad into the world of usability experts. You'll learn about their motivations, terminology, and strategies for judging the success (or failure) of an application. My hope is, with this knowledge, you'll have a greater confidence to begin studying users in a more meaningful way.

The industry of human–computer interaction is vast, with decades of scientific research. We couldn't possibly cover every aspect of what is known about usability today. However, this book is full of great (and practical) examples to help you get started.

With this book you'll learn:

- How to implement user-centered design and usability practices
- How to deal with different types of users and their unique personalities
- How to create a vision that's essential to your application's success
- How to create a plan that will help you navigate the development process and avoid costly mistakes

- How to boost creativity and create engaging applications using common design principles
- How to gather feedback and make informed design decisions

Throughout our discussion, I'll share tools and processes I've found helpful in my own work. While the various technology, stories, and examples used in this book may become dated or obsolete, the lessons we learn from them will not.

Perhaps you're a lone developer, building mobile applications for a broad consumer base. Maybe you're working with a small development team, creating line-of-business applications for your organization. Maybe you've started programming as a hobby in hopes of making it a full-time career. Many of us don't have access to a UX professional or designer on our team. We're left to figure it out for ourselves. Although, the value of UX and its associated methodologies are becoming more realized, many organizations aren't quite ready to invest in full-time positions.

It's not just enterprise developers either. Through our weekly Internet show, I've talked with many developers who are building applications without any formal design or usability training. Often times, they learn enough to get by but continue to struggle with the fundamentals of creating a great user experience.

In any of these situations, the information in this book will help you build better applications by strengthening your observation and design skills.

The book is broken down into the following concepts:

What is user-centered design?
> To begin, we'll have a discussion about the relationships and common misconceptions regarding usability, user-centered design, and user experience.

Working with users
> We'll talk about strategies to get the most from your users.

Having a plan
> Building a successful application (a successful *anything*, for that matter) requires thoughtful planning. We'll cover critical steps that should be included in your development process. These items will help you implement user feedback effectively.

Creating a personal manifesto
> One thing becomes clear when talking to successful developers and designers. They each have a clear vision of what they want to achieve with their applications. We'll discuss why having a vision is the key to creating a meaningful product.

Creativity and user experience
> It takes creative insight to continually generate ideas to solve users' needs. We'll talk about ways you can boost your own creativity and inspiration.

Design principles

Fortunately for us, many principles exist to guide us towards proven designs that work. We'll discuss some of the most popular design principles you can apply to your applications to dramatically improve their usability.

Gathering feedback

Collecting meaningful data from users is the crux of user-centered design. We'll talk about the different methods researchers employ to solve user-experience concerns.

Usability studies

Observing users while they use your applications is one of the most important processes in usability research. We'll discuss the various tools needed to conduct your own studies.

Conventions Used in This Book

The following typographical conventions are used in this book:

Italic

Indicates new terms, URLs, email addresses, filenames, and file extensions.

`Constant width`

Used for program listings, as well as within paragraphs to refer to program elements such as variable or function names, databases, data types, environment variables, statements, and keywords.

`Constant width bold`

Shows commands or other text that should be typed literally by the user.

`Constant width italic`

Shows text that should be replaced with user-supplied values or by values determined by context.

This icon signifies a tip, suggestion, or general note.

This icon indicates a warning or caution.

Using Code Examples

This book is here to help you get your job done. In general, if this book includes code examples, you may use the code in your programs and documentation. You do not need to contact us for permission unless you're reproducing a significant portion of the code. For example, writing a program that uses several chunks of code from this book does not require permission. Selling or distributing a CD-ROM of examples from O'Reilly books does require permission. Answering a question by citing this book and quoting example code does not require permission. Incorporating a significant amount of example code from this book into your product's documentation does require permission.

We appreciate, but do not require, attribution. An attribution usually includes the title, author, publisher, and ISBN. For example: "*User-Centered Design* by Travis Lowdermilk (O'Reilly). Copyright 2013 Travis Lowdermilk, 978-1-449-35980-5."

If you feel your use of code examples falls outside fair use or the permission given above, feel free to contact us at *permissions@oreilly.com*.

Safari® Books Online

 Safari Books Online (*www.safaribooksonline.com*) is an on-demand digital library that delivers expert content in both book and video form from the world's leading authors in technology and business.

Technology professionals, software developers, web designers, and business and creative professionals use Safari Books Online as their primary resource for research, problem solving, learning, and certification training.

Safari Books Online offers a range of product mixes and pricing programs for organizations, government agencies, and individuals. Subscribers have access to thousands of books, training videos, and prepublication manuscripts in one fully searchable database from publishers like O'Reilly Media, Prentice Hall Professional, Addison-Wesley Professional, Microsoft Press, Sams, Que, Peachpit Press, Focal Press, Cisco Press, John Wiley & Sons, Syngress, Morgan Kaufmann, IBM Redbooks, Packt, Adobe Press, FT Press, Apress, Manning, New Riders, McGraw-Hill, Jones & Bartlett, Course Technology, and dozens more. For more information about Safari Books Online, please visit us online.

How to Contact Us

Please address comments and questions concerning this book to the publisher:

O'Reilly Media, Inc.
1005 Gravenstein Highway North
Sebastopol, CA 95472

800-998-9938 (in the United States or Canada)
707-829-0515 (international or local)
707-829-0104 (fax)

We have a web page for this book, where we list errata, examples, and any additional information. You can access this page at *http://oreil.ly/user-centered-design*.

To comment or ask technical questions about this book, send email to *bookquestions@oreilly.com*.

For more information about our books, courses, conferences, and news, see our website at *http://www.oreilly.com*.

Find us on Facebook: *http://facebook.com/oreilly*

Follow us on Twitter: *http://twitter.com/oreillymedia*

Watch us on YouTube: *http://www.youtube.com/oreillymedia*

Acknowledgments

People Who Helped Me Write This Book

These individuals were gracious enough to spend some time with me so I could share their knowledge with you. Like I've written in this book, in order to be great, you need to follow great people. In my opinion, these are some of the greatest:

Julian Walker

Lead engineer at FiftyThree and creator of Paper. If you want to see more of what Julian is up to, follow him on Twitter @julianwalker.

Jeff Weir

UX Designer for Microsoft who has worked with the Windows and Live Labs teams. You can find talks that Jeff has presented on Channel 9 (*http://msdn.channel9.com*), Microsoft's video site for developers.

Billy Hollis

A developer-evangelist who promotes the value of good usability practices. Billy is well known in the Microsoft .NET developer community and has his own consulting company called Next Version Systems.

Robby Ingebretsen

A UX Designer and founder of Pixel Lab, a Seattle software design and strategy firm. You can find all about Robby on Twitter @ingebretsen or at his personal blog (*http://thinkpixellab.com*).

Mark and Lisa

This book would not be in your hands if it weren't for the guidance and sheer genius of these two. Go Blue Demons!

Mary Treseler and the O'Reilly Media Family

This book is an example of the notion that the industry of application development is changing. Kudos to the entire team at O'Reilly Media for helping others and me learn about the importance of great usability and design. O'Reilly continues to prove themselves as a guiding rod for developers by helping them stay ahead of this ever-changing landscape.

Mary, thanks for being super cool and making me feel like a legitimate author, something that is really weird when I say it out loud.

Amanda, your sharp eye and wisdom have made this book much better than I could've ever imagined. Thank you.

Thanks to the many reviewers who offered their thoughtful opinions and insight.

People Who Helped Me with Life

My parents

Kim, Deborah, Kathi, Joe, David, and John. Thanks for all the love and support. This book is as much your achievement as it is mine.

My brothers

The best bunch of bros out there: Ryan, Brandon, and Brett—thank you for always having my back.

My sister

Hope, you get your own section because you're my favorite sister. Hugs.

My good friends

JC, Daniel, Matt, and Travis (and their wives and kids, too)! V-Town, baby!

One of my sweetest friends, Margery Godfrey. I kept my promise.

My coworkers

The entire staff of Kaweah Delta Health Care District: Dave, Nick, Steven, Eli, Mark, Anita, and Tim—thanks for putting up with my incessant ramblings. Most of what's in this book came from your patience and active feedback.

My boys

Noah and Jackson, let this little book be a testament to the power of hard work and determination. You're in my heart and on my mind always.

My wife

Jackie, as with all things in my life, this book begins and ends with you. Thank you for all your hard work and support. This life couldn't have happened without you.

CHAPTER 1
Our World Has Changed

*"Standing still is the fastest way of moving
backwards in a rapidly changing world."*

—Lauren Bacall

On January 9, 2007, a man quietly walked onto a stage and changed the course of technological history. He announced that his company was about to launch a product that would forever change the way we communicate.

Then, in a dramatic fashion, he held up a phone he and his company had been working on for over five years. Reporters furiously captured images of the device, quickly sending them to every corner of the world. The man demonstrated how you could zoom out on images by making a pinching gesture and navigate your music library by swiping a single finger across the screen. He walked through various applications: a notepad, calendar, compass, and detailed maps. No one had seen anything like it. The phone seemed like a product of science fiction. But it was very real, and all of it was small enough to fit into your pocket.

Back then, I worked as a web programmer for a children's hospital. I remember sitting at my desk watching the demonstration via a live blog and waiting what seemed like forever for the images to stream to my computer. As soon as I saw the first picture of the iPhone, I remember feeling as though I'd just witnessed something significant. At that moment, I hadn't yet realized the extent of the iPhone's impact on our industry; but as a developer, I could see that the bar had been raised. I knew the days of getting a pass for cluttered user interface (UI) and confusing layouts were over.

My users were going to expect more.

It wasn't enough that my applications had fast load times or a laundry list of features. My users were going to want the iPhone. Not just the product specifically, but what it represented. It was intuitive, minimal, and engaging; and now my users had a shining example of how everything should work. New forms of interaction were ushered into the conversation, and terms like Multi-Touch and NUI instantly became part of developers' lingua franca.

A year later, Apple opened the App Store for the iPhone, creating an explosion of application development. Developers began competing in saturated markets where users had thousands of choices, and in most cases, *hundreds* of thousands. Companies like Google, Microsoft, Facebook, and Amazon were also growing their extensive development platforms.

Today, more and more consumers are purchasing these products and services. They've become reliant on them and they bring them into the workplace. IT departments are no longer controlling their environments by issuing phones and computers; the expectation is that all these devices just work on the user's corporate network. Therefore, the bar has been raised for the enterprise developer, too. Corporate users expect things like company portals and line-of-business applications to be thoughtfully designed and engaging, just like the products they use at home.

So, as developers, how do we cope with all of this?

I have a rather simple presumption. In order to build products that users love, we need to include users in the process of building them. Granted, many might point to Steve Jobs as the antithesis of what I'm suggesting. In a May 1998 article by *Bloomberg Business Week*, Jobs famously said:

> It's really hard to design products by focus groups. A lot of times, people don't know what they want until you show it to them.

While some of this sentiment may be true, I think we have to be honest with ourselves. Jobs had a unique ability to understand what users wanted, and many of us don't possess that ability:

> We've always tried to be at the intersection of technology and liberal arts, to be able to get the best of both, to make extremely advanced products from a technology point of view, but also have them be intuitive, easy to use, fun to use, so that they really fit the users—the users don't have to come to them, they come to the user.

I don't believe Jobs could've created products that met the "intersection of technology and liberal arts" without understanding the wide spectrum of users' needs. We can't build products that "come to the user" if we're unwilling to come to the user ourselves. While Apple may have an intuitive understanding of human behavior, many developers do not.

However, I do believe this type of intuition can be acquired over time, and the best way to acquire it is by spending time with users.

By collecting feedback and observing their behavior, we can gain valuable insights into building applications they'll love. Anyone involved in the process of creating an application (not just designers) should be invested in understanding what users need to complete the application's purpose. It's more than just graphic design, code, or functionality. It's the entire team (or just you) continually working to understand the user. Not all of our users' problems can be solved with code, although I wish they could be; therefore, developers need to take a more holistic approach.

This notion might seem like common sense, but it still amazes me how many developers aren't taking the time to do this.

Most of my experiences come from working in a community hospital setting. It's a uniquely different world than other software development environments; however, I still encounter many of the same challenges. In a hospital setting, users are treated just like clients. They make a request for our services, we sit down with them and outline how we plan to help, and then we deliver a product (fingers crossed!) by the agreed upon deadline.

We've been able to improve our process by implementing the user-centered design practices outlined in this book. By focusing on usability, we save time and create applications that meet our users' needs. Although our development environment may be different than yours, you'll find that the practices detailed in this book can be modified to meet your needs or circumstances.

This book isn't a lengthy tome on the history or current state of usability. It's meant to be a collection of sensible tools and methods that you can start implementing today. This isn't a magical formula that, when applied, produces a perfect application. Ideally, you'll come away from our discussion with your own views and ideas of how to improve your development process and re-engage your users.

Being a developer myself, I realize that we're in a nonstop world of ever-changing frameworks, coding languages, and whiz-bang editing tools. It can seem daunting to add more steps to your development life cycle.

However, the methods described in this book are essential in creating a focused and efficient development process. These steps will actually save you time and prevent your projects from heading in the wrong direction.

I know some developers measure a book's value by its page count, but this book is smaller by design. I've done my best to create a high-level overview so you can get started quickly. Be sure to review "The Short Version" at the end of each chapter. These are bulleted lists that summarize the main concepts of each section.

It's an exciting time to be a developer! There are so many ways we can enrich people's lives. We have the ability to delight them and change the way they interact with the world and each other. It's a unique and challenging responsibility.

After our discussion, I hope you'll have an even greater desire to explore the user experience community. Be sure to check out Chapter 11 for useful links for industry thought-leaders, publications, and products to help you along the way.

Now, let's get started!

CHAPTER 2

What Is User-Centered Design?

"Ease of use may be invisible,
but its absence sure isn't."

—IBM

The most common and misguided presumption I find, especially within the developer community, is that the practice of usability is just subjective. These developers believe that usability decisions are arbitrary and can be decided by simply applying their own personal preference. Additionally, many of these decisions are made for reasons that have nothing to do with users. You better believe the CEO's current missive lands on the home page of the company portal. Who cares if it was written in lime green and has a dancing chili pepper on top? Therefore, if you're developing an application with a team or within an enterprise environment, you might be challenged when trying to implement user-centered design.

Perhaps you feel like you're the only member of your team who cares about the user's experience. Your colleagues or peers might roll their eyes when you talk about the importance of good layout and design. I realize this can be a long and lonesome journey, but it doesn't have to be. There are ways to spread sound, user-centered knowledge to disarm even your most vocal critics. One way to do this is by educating your team or organization about the value of user-centered design. To do that, we need to understand what user-centered design is; and most importantly, what it is not.

UCD Is Not Usability

I realize that my interchangeable use of user-centered design and usability might create confusion. Usability, also referred to as human factors, is the study of how humans relate to any product. Usability practices could be implemented in everything from a toaster to a doorknob, and even the packaging of both.

Human–computer interaction (HCI) is rooted in usability, but it focuses on how humans relate to computing products.

User-centered design (UCD) emerged from HCI and is a software design methodology for developers and designers. Essentially, it helps them make applications that meet the needs of their users.

Although this may be a bit of an over-simplification, Figure 2-1 is a diagram to help you understand the relationship between these methodologies.

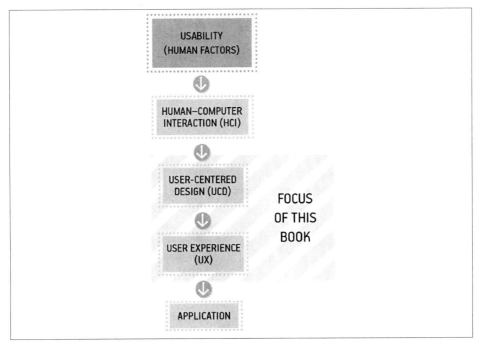

Figure 2-1. The relationship between usability, HCI, UCD, and UX

It's fair to say that practicing user-centered design will ensure that your application maintains good usability. That's the whole point! By placing users at the center of your development process, you remove ambiguity and get to the heart of what they need.

Additionally, there is the subject of user experience (UX). UX is a term often used to summarize the entire experience of a software product. It not only encompasses functionality, but also how engaging and delightful an application is to use. An application's UX is greater than the sum of its parts.

User-centered design can be implemented to ensure that your application maintains a great user experience.

UCD Is Not Subjective

The entire discipline of usability, and all of its underlying methodologies, is a conglomeration of many scientific disciplines. Through the implementation of ergonomics, psychology, anthropology, and many other fields, usability is rooted in scientific knowledge. It's far from subjective thinking or conjecture.

The user-centered design process works *against* subjective assumptions about user behavior. It requires proof that your design decisions are effective. If user-centered design is done correctly, your application becomes an outcome of actively engaging users. Therefore, any design decisions that were made by observing and listening to them will not be based on whims or personal preferences.

As the saying goes, "numbers don't lie." The user-centered design practice relies on data to support your design decisions. One way to do this is by completing usability studies (see Chapter 9). By observing users directly, we remove assumptions and statistically prove what is actually happening. This gives us a more stable foundation for the direction of our development.

Effectively, the data collected throughout the user-centered design process should make it difficult to argue against the changes your application needs.

UCD Is Not Just Design

This is probably the most common misunderstanding about user-centered design. Some people (and I find this mostly amongst our developer friends) believe that user-centered design practitioners are only focused on aesthetics or making things look pretty. While an application's aesthetic can be important, it's not the whole picture.

Being user-focused is more than just deliberating on how things look or creating flashy animations and slick transitions. User-centered design ensures that we examine how effective an application is in achieving its designed purpose. It's possible, as Figure 2-2 shows, to have a stunningly beautiful application that's a usability nightmare.

Of course, the reverse could be true. A usability study can identify flaws in your application's user interface (UI) that make it difficult to complete tasks. In this case, your application's UI plays a huge role in achieving success; however, it would be a mistake to make it our only focus.

Figure 2-2. The designers of this bicycle should have conducted a usability study!

UCD Is Not a Waste of Time or Money

Dedicating time to proper user-centered design practices can be a difficult thing to do. The very nature of UCD requires reflection and observation. Let's face it, if you're spending your development time reflecting on design choices, it can feel like you're not moving forward. Also, if your usability research reveals design problems, you may end up having to remove previous efforts. That can feel like you're moving backwards!

User-centered design requires that we ask users what they don't like about our applications. Sometimes we don't want to hear their criticisms, or we assume we know what they're going to say. Opening up to feedback means opening up to complaints, and no one wants to hear how terrible of a job he's doing. Sure, Sally was just being "constructive" when she said your application was "worthless."

To avoid these criticisms, we ignore our users and shut them out. We focus on finishing our code, hoping all the other things will just sort themselves out.

Listen, I get it. As developers, the toolset of knowledge we must become familiar with is always expanding. New technologies emerge, form factors change, and new coding frameworks spring up daily. One minute, you've got a complex set of APIs all figured out, and the next minute you're reading a blog article about how it's dead, with a brand new API taking its place!

Getting into the business of being a programmer is to forever agree that you're constantly learning; and as technologies become more complicated, it requires more of our time and investment. With all of these challenges, the temptation is to dive deeper into our code and shut out any "distractions" like usability testing.

Billy Hollis, a developer-evangelist who promotes the value of usability practices, says that this resistance is a big challenge for our industry. He suggests the developer community loses valuable leaders in the usability space because they can't balance learning new coding techniques and spending time with users. They end up having to choose one over the other. Therefore, the community is full of code-only developers willing to spend their entire focus on learning the next API:

> I think that's one of the reasons we see such tremendous resistance [from developers] to design. The very people who've survived in the developer ecosystem are the ones who love code so much that they shut everything else out.

The point of user-centered design is that it doesn't have to be an either/or. Involving users' feedback in your development process can be a powerful both/and. Also, you don't need to be a user experience expert to implement good usability principles.

Hollis likens the process to learning how to ski:

> When you set out to ski, you're not trying to learn to become an Olympic skier. You're trying to learn to get to the bottom of the hill without falling down.

We have to break through the mindset that if we're not writing code, then our application isn't progressing. We need to accept that time spent with our users is a necessary part of the development process. It's just as necessary as learning and writing code. It seems that some developers spend more time deciding what framework they're going to use than how they plan to provide value for their users. It's as if these developers assume their application idea is inherently valuable.

If implemented correctly, user-centered design can actually *save you time*. By making sure you understand users' needs, you eliminate misunderstandings and costly mistakes. Remember, rebuilding your application because you didn't meet your users' expectations is a waste of time, too!

I would argue that problem solving outside of code would expose you to new ways of critical thinking. Taking a break from your code and conducting a survey or usability study can allow you to look at the problem from a different angle. You may find that when you return to your code, you're more focused and directed about what needs to be improved.

You may have the desire to conduct user research, but it doesn't seem financially viable to do so. After all, time is money; therefore, the perception is that time spent on anything other than writing code is costly.

Producing evidence of the return on investment (ROI) of user-centered design is outside the scope of our discussion; however, I would encourage you to think of usability as a way to avoid *losing* money. Fixing production bugs and supporting users through confusing and broken workflows requires a significant financial commitment as well.

In an article published in *interactions* magazine, Arnold Lund makes a similar case:

> An alternative approach is to view usability testing as part of a software quality management program and to justify it through the reduction in costs that would otherwise be incurred if usability bugs were not removed early in development. These costs include support costs for deployed software and the costs of fixing software once it is deployed.

If you're having trouble convincing management (or yourself) on the financial benefits of embracing user-centered design methodologies, consider making a financial case from another angle like cost avoidance.

UCD Is Not a Bug Report

You might believe that you're already performing user-centered design by simply giving users the ability to submit a bug or issue within your application.

While this is admirable and certainly something you should continue doing, do not substitute bug reports for comprehensive user research.

By continually looking at user feedback as a task list of items that need to be fixed, you never get to the root of what your users need.

Suppose a user submits a bug report for a feature that is not working correctly. You may be tempted to immediately drill into your code, find the source of the issue, and fix it as soon as possible.

If you're not taking the time to question what the user was trying to achieve when they encountered the issue, you gain no meaningful insight into how you could improve the application as a whole.

By exploring and asking questions that are unrelated to specific bugs, you might discover that users are trying to use your application in a way that you didn't realize. You might consider rewriting features to make those workflows more clear, or, better yet, the discussion could generate new ideas on how your application could provide more value.

Once I received a support ticket because a user was encountering an error every time she tried to submit a record in my application. The ticket provided all the technical details, including the entire error message. I thought I was so clever to include automated bug reporting within my application. Every time a user encountered an error, a ticket was automatically generated and sent to me. No more wasted time having to talk with users! Big mistake.

For hours I dug into the code and tried to discover a syntax or programming logic error. I looked through all my database connections and even reviewed the databases themselves. I reviewed the error message in the automated ticket several times.

Finally, feeling like I was getting nowhere, I decided to call the user. I asked her what she was trying to do. It turned out that the cause of the error was because she was including some invalid characters in a comments field on one of the application's forms.

Admittedly, it should've occurred to me that a user might input these special characters, and I should've conditioned my code to allow it. However, the larger issue was that she was trying to use a general comments field to document important medical information.

After spending some more time with the user, I realized that I needed to create more fields on the form to capture the information she was trying to document. My automated bug report was not the complete picture of the issue. If I had missed the opportunity to speak with the user by just fixing the problem within the code and moving on, I would have been unaware of her need for additional documentation.

Thus, users would've continued to use a general comments field to document vital medical information.

This is why the totality of your user feedback should not be just a list of errors within your application. Consider using bug reports only as a way to augment your overall user-design strategy.

UCD Is Not a Distraction

Have you ever been in a meeting listening to your users' requests, and your mind drifts to the dreamy land of the solution?

- Should I use a web service, or should I connect directly to the data?
- I wonder if we could build this on our company portal.
- What programming language should I use?
- I bet I could build this as a module on top of our main product.
- I'd love to use this as an opportunity to finally build a mobile application.

All of this technical thinking is fine. However, it has no bearing on what clients need because we haven't collected their user requirements yet! User-centered design helps us remain focused on the user's core needs. It ensures that we get solid information first and prevents us from trying to make the problem fit the technology.

Granted, there are real technological constraints that we have to deal with, but developers often make the mistake of addressing those issues first. User-centered design helps us move properly from our users' requirements to our technological solution. It's a purposeful approach that makes sure that we complete tasks in the proper order. We'll talk more about this process in Chapter 4.

For now, understand that usability is not a distraction. In fact, it actually works against distractions by helping you focus on the right things. It puts you in the correct mindset so that you can ask the right questions and challenge any preconceived notions.

Rather than contemplating technology, here are some questions we should be asking first:

- What is the source of the user's request? Can a technical solution solve his problem? Perhaps his problem is procedural or even political. Maybe it's a process, workflow, or education issue.
- Why is the user confused about this message? How does he interpret its meaning? Should I explain it a different way?
- Why does the user get lost between these two screens?
- Why did he miss this alert? Is he just ignoring it? If so, why?
- Why is the user completing tasks in the wrong order? Is there a better way to organize the layout to ensure he does it the right way?

A common theme throughout the study of usability is asking *why*. User-centered design helps us to become hyperfocused on understanding user behavior. It's a framework to help us discover the most effective response to their needs.

By combining usability, user-centered design, and user experience, you're ensuring a more complete approach to your application's development. It requires focus, determination, and even a little sacrifice. However, ignoring these aspects of your application, especially in today's ever-competitive market, is doing yourself and your users a disservice.

The Short Version

- The world of usability is broad and focuses on the study of humans interacting with *any* product.

- Human–computer interaction (HCI) is a subset of usability that focuses specifically on humans interacting with *computing* products.

- User-centered design (UCD) is a methodology used by developers and designers to ensure they're creating products that meet users' needs.

- User experience (UX) is one of the many focuses of UCD. It includes the user's entire experience with the product, including physical and emotional reactions.

- UCD is not subjective and often relies on data to support design decisions.

- UCD involves much more than making applications aesthetically pleasing. Design plays an important role; however, it's not the only focus.

- UCD can actually save time by helping you avoid costly mistakes.

- UCD doesn't distract us from getting work done. It ensures that we focus on the right things: meeting users' needs with the proper technological solution.

CHAPTER 3

Working with Users

> *"Coming together is a beginning. Keeping together is progress. Working together is success."*
>
> —Henry Ford

I realize that involving users can be a scary thing. Let's face it: users have a tendency to muddy up our development processes; they don't understand what's required to build an application; and most of the time they have no idea what they're asking for. Sometimes, their requests are unrealistic and unhelpful. How could they possibly lead us to any sort of meaningful breakthrough on a software project?

It's becoming increasingly clear that the job of a developer exceeds the realm of writing code. We have to be more attuned to our users' needs, and the only way to do that is to spend time with them. We have to constructively guide our users so they provide us with (whether they realize it or not) the information we need to make a successful application.

This requires us to do more listening by remaining observant and inquisitive.

What If I Don't Have Access to Users?

Many of you could be reading this and thinking to yourself, "I don't have a group of users that I'm directly working with." Maybe you're building something for the mass market, like a smartphone application or website. If that's the case, you may be confused when I start talking about engaging users and actively working with them.

Here's my advice: if you're not building an application for a specific client or group of users, then I'd encourage you to find some. Perhaps this seems obvious, but I've seen many developers set out to build an application assuming, if they just build it, users will come. These developers put very little effort into understanding whom those users might be and what their needs are.

At the end of the day, the application you're building should be serving *someone*. The trick is finding people that personify who that someone is. I find social networks like Twitter and Facebook are great ways to find friends or family willing to offer feedback or answer questions.

Granted, the process is not as straightforward as building an application for a client or in an enterprise environment, but the principles of user-centered design still hold true. The key is making sure users are involved, at some level, in your software design choices. This is the best way to ensure you're building an application people want and need.

Some developers might limit their interaction with users and choose to go with their gut. To a certain extent this is admirable, but it's not the most effective way to make decisions about your application's design. That's not to say there hasn't been evidence of developers using their own intuition to make successful products. We've seen countless examples of developers who have pioneered revolutionary software and services, simply by having the foresight and intuition to decide what was needed. They didn't need a focus group or extensive market study. They just *knew* that the application should be built.

I've revised a quote from Steve Furtick, pastor of the Elevation church in North Carolina, and I think it best qualifies my response. *Don't compare someone's highlight reel to your behind-the-scenes video.*

In other words, it's easy to look at products like Google, Facebook, Twitter, Amazon, Groupon, (and on and on) and think that creating software is all about the big idea. We mistakenly believe that, like Newton, an apple fell from a tree and plunked these developers on their heads, magically ushering in a digital revolution. So I see developers waiting for the apple to hit them, too, and I think to myself, "You know, if they just spent some time with people, they'd probably get there faster."

If we've seen only the high points of someone's application and none of the mistakes, it's easy for us to believe the developer just happened on a great idea.

Leonardo da Vinci, for instance, had notebooks full of sketches and drawings for his final work on *The Last Supper*. He didn't just sit down one day and paint his masterpiece. He spent years sketching, erasing, and redrawing different ideas and concepts, as is depicted in Figure 3-1. Most of us aren't even aware of these early sketches; all we hear about is the final painting that has been adored by millions.

Figure 3-1. Early drawings from Leonardo da Vinci for The Last Supper

So the point is this: don't mistake the process of creating a user-centered application as a straight line from A to B. It can take years of observation and study to lead you to your breakthrough moment. Your process should be a curvy line from A to B to E, back to A, and moved so many times you lose track.

If you're willing to spend time asking questions, being curious about the world around you, and observing user behavior, you increase your chances of gaining insight. Over time, that insight will expand your intuition and, quite possibly, lead you to a successful product.

Knowing When to Listen to Users and When to Not

Just because I'm suggesting that we listen to users does not mean that we should listen to *everything* they tell us. This is not like the retail experience where the customer is always right. Most users have no idea how technology works. They don't know what's possible or impossible. Sometimes their ideas are just plain crazy; however, if they are carefully guided, their knowledge can be extremely valuable. At the end of the day, we need to learn what to hold onto and what to throw out.

One morning, I was walking by a visitor kiosk I had built for our front lobby. The kiosk allowed our visitors to locate the patients they were visiting within the hospital. It also had locations of various points of interest. I saw a woman and her daughter using the kiosk and decided to use the opportunity to question the woman about her experience"

> "Hi, my name is Travis. I work here at the hospital. I was wondering if you were able to use the kiosk OK."
>
> "Oh yes! I mean, my daughter had to help me at first, but I think it's really cool!"
>
> "Great; were you able to locate the patient OK?"
>
> "Yes. We found my dad. You know what would be great? If the tiles in the floor lit up and took us where we could find him!"

Now, this may shock you, but I wasn't able to create a system that caused the floor to light up. Frankly, if I could do that, I'd probably be living on a beach somewhere collecting my millions. This was a ludicrous idea. Clearly the woman had no idea how technology worked or what I was capable of delivering.

However, she had touched on an interesting problem. It's difficult for users to take information from a computer directory and translate it to the world around them. In other words, I was presenting the room number and floor, but there needed to be a clear indication of where to go next.

Throughout the development, I had already anticipated this problem and created a series of animations using dots and a map of the floor. Much like her idea of a light-up floor, these animations, shown in Figure 3-2, lead the visitor to the nearest elevator.

Therefore, this woman's outrageous request had validated my earlier assumptions and caused me to reflect on the value of the animations. Sure, the floor wasn't lighting up, but a map with animated dots was the next best thing.

What most users provide is the understanding of their own workflows. It's up to you to explain how you can augment those workflows with your programming skills. It'll be your job to educate them and bring them into your process. Teach them the right terminology so they can adequately explain their needs.

Through active listening and coaching, you can guide users into giving you the information you're looking for. You have to ask the right questions, and if you're not getting what you need, you have to ask them a different way. Be persistent.

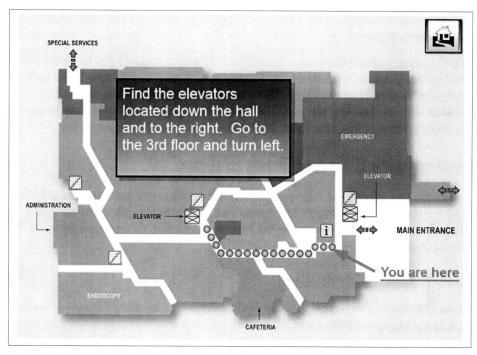

Figure 3-2. Visitor directory with animated dots leading to the nearest elevator

In the past, I've spent 30 minutes on just one question to ensure I've received the proper information. If a user is giving me something I don't need, I'll politely explain how that information doesn't help. If a user is explaining something I don't understand, I'll tell her. I don't hide the fact that I have no idea how her task or process works. When I let my guard down and admit that I don't have all the answers, not only does it take the pressure off me, but it also makes me more relatable to the user.

In *Observing the User Experience* (Morgan Kaufmann), author Mike Kuniavsky describes this as the *master/apprentice model*. In this model, you treat the user as the master craftswoman who is focused on providing you all the necessary details of what she's doing.

This is particularly useful in jobs or industries that you're unfamiliar with. If you were building a scheduling application for a veterinarian's office, it would make sense to have you shadow the office receptionist.

I encounter this at the hospital all the time. As much as I might wish I was a doctor, even after all these years, I still don't have enough terminology to star as an extra in *Grey's Anatomy*. Every day, I'm learning new workflows, acronyms (so many acronyms), or services our hospital provides. I'm never too shy to admit I don't know what a user is talking about. Through a series of questioning, I'll get her to describe her workflow in a way I can understand.

I think programmers often come with a stigma of being all-knowing or beyond normal intelligence. Users can sometimes feel intimidated. A great way to open them up is to be the first to admit you need help. This puts users in the right frame of mind. They're the ones with the answers, not you. Their job is to help you learn what they do so you can build a better product for them. That's how user-centered design works!

Dealing with Different Types of Users

There's no one solution to help you get the information you need from users. Each person has a different way of tackling problems. You have to be flexible and willing to adapt to differing approaches and styles. Here are some common personality types I've come across:

The Information Overloader

These users like to give you information—a lot of information. They'll come to meetings with stacks of papers and memos. They'll copy you on emails with long threads, giving you no context as to why you've been included. They'll explain the entire history of their process with great detail and even include a story about their first vacation to Hawaii. They'll give you copies of notes they've taken from every meeting they've ever attended. They'll call you about an idea for version 2, even though you haven't started building version 1. Their heart is in the right place, but they don't understand that you can't keep up with the amount of information they're giving you.

The challenge with these types of users is that you don't want to discourage them. If the problem is that they're giving you *too much information* then, in reality, that's a great problem to have! With that said, you have to set boundaries for the information you'll consider. Coach them in the proper ways to communicate with you.

If you'd rather not receive phone calls, let them know it would be best to communicate nonurgent items over email. If they're still calling, let them go to voice mail. Then, politely and promptly, respond to their message with an email. This is a great way to coach them into using the preferred forms of communication.

If they want to start talking about the next version, explain to them the importance of staying focused on the current version. These types of users have a tendency to get ahead of themselves, so continually bring them back to the task at hand.

I find that providing status updates via email is a great way to remind them of what you're focusing on. I create recurring calendar appointments to make sure I'm continually providing users updated information about their projects. This is a more proactive approach where I'm contacting them before they feel the need to check in with me. It also helps to schedule time to stop and reflect on what's been accomplished and what still needs to be done.

Most likely, users' willingness to help is a result of just being excited. They're finally getting help, and they want to make sure you have everything you need. As my father-in-law says, "Sometimes, you have to let them get their words out." Be patient with them and try to be thankful they're willing to provide information. Remember, at the end of the day, they're your customers, and they should be respected accordingly.

The Control Freak

Control Freaks want to be involved in every decision on the project. They exert their presence in meetings and will often derail presentations or discussions. They'll complain when they don't run things or when the group decides to go in a different direction. In short, these users want to be the ones calling the shots. They want to tell you how it's all going to be done.

My experience is that the need for control comes from a sense of insecurity. If you're willing, try to get to the center of what they're concerned about. You might try having a private meeting and let them know what you're trying to achieve. Remind them that your desire is to make the best application possible. Give them examples of how they can help you and remind them that you're on the same team!

Choose your battles and let them make decisions on things that have little impact. Also, it's best to present choices before letting them decide. By limiting their options, you can minimize their overall influence.

Sometimes they just want to feel included and respected. Make sure to prompt them for their opinion during meetings and politely move on when things get off track. Your job is to make sure you hear from everyone. Don't be afraid to mediate during meetings if one person is taking over.

More often than not, these users end up being your best allies because they can be incredibly knowledgeable. At the hospital, we have special users we refer to as super users. These are folks who we partner with to achieve better outcomes. If you build applications for the mass market, think about establishing a beta program where some of your more vocal users can use unreleased or test versions of your product.

For the super user, the role may come with additional responsibilities and a greater expectation of involvement. I find that this elevation of engagement works very well for this type of personality.

Unlike the master/apprentice model, this is referred to as the *partnership model*. These users have the ability to examine their own (or others') usability behaviors and make assessments on what may be needed. Rather than just being another user to be observed, they can actually help in developing and implementing your user-centered design strategy. Because they are more intimately involved in the outcome of the process, you may find that they back off and become more of a team player.

The Devil's Advocate

"That won't work."

"We've already tried that."

"If you change the menu, no one will use it!"

Devil's Advocates have a hard time coming up with their own ideas, but they'll gladly tell you why yours won't work. By playing the role of the Devil's Advocate, it allows them to tear apart your idea while not being the bad guy. After all, it's not them saying it. They're just advocating on behalf of the Devil.

In *The Ten Faces of Innovation: IDEO's Strategies for Beating the Devil's Advocate and Driving Creativity Throughout Your Organization* (Doubleday), author Tom Kelley explains how to encourage more constructive personalities on your team and minimize the effect of the Devil's Advocate.

By giving users (or team members) detailed roles to play, you're empowering them to participate in a specific way. Each persona is responsible for an aspect of the creative process.

For example, the role of the Anthropologist is responsible for observing human behaviors and reporting back to the group. The Experimenter tests new ideas and validates assumptions. The Cross-Pollinator explores other industries and cultures and then translates her findings into new insights.

You may have people on your team who naturally fit these personas, or you might have to employ one person to fill many personas. The key to Kelley's model is giving each member a defined character or role to play. Each person will then have a responsibility to represent her view from the perspective of her role. Therefore, it makes less sense for someone to be against an idea, simply because she's playing the role of someone who disagrees. That role just doesn't exist. The Devil's Advocate becomes marginalized by the stronger points of view.

In his book, Kelley details the roles and responsibilities of each of the ten personas and, although they might not completely eliminate the Devil's Advocate, they certainly help. After all, it's not the person who is disagreeing with the Devil's Advocate; it's the persona she's been given:

> The Devil's Advocate may never go away, but the ten personas can keep him in his place. Or tell him to go to hell.

So, instead of hearing, "Let me play the Devil's Advocate for a minute; if we change the menu system, our users will be confused and frustrated," you'll hear, "Let me play the Anthropologist for a minute. I've been watching our users with the current menu system, and they're already confused and frustrated!"

Dealing with Negativity

Working with users isn't always easy, especially if they want to focus only on what's wrong. Developers are required to have a thick skin: you can't be in this business if you refuse to be criticized. However, we have to admit that negativity reduces our morale and motivation.

Our job is to remain optimistic. We have to have faith that we can provide the solution our users need. We must believe the answer is waiting to be discovered, and with enough persistence, we can uncover it. That's not to say that we should be delusional or unrealistic, but I think we have to actively work against the negative mindset.

To be honest, it's much easier to make a list of what's going wrong than what's going right. We're kind of wired to think that way. As developers, part of our job is to focus on errors in our code and processes that aren't working. We search and root out failure by eliminating bugs. Unfortunately, we end up applying the same focus to every situation by mistaking a problem as a collection of bugs to be fixed. In turn, we become hyper-focused on what's not working.

Instead, we might consider taking time to actively look at what *is working*.

Let me be clear. I'm not suggesting that looking for mistakes is a bad thing. We should always remain focused on finding errors or things that aren't working. It's essential to the software development process. However, I think we can balance our time to include the evaluation of things that are working. There's a lot to learn from our mistakes, but there's a lot we can learn from our successes, too.

In the book *Switch: How to Change Things When Change is Hard* (Crown Business), authors Chip and Dan Heath refer to this shift in focus as "finding the bright spots." Essentially, they believe that motivation and change come from focusing on what's *working* and not what's *failing*:

> Imagine a world in which you experienced a rush of gratitude every single time you flipped a light switch and the room lit up. Imagine a world in which after a husband forgot his wife's birthday, she gave him a big kiss and said, "For thirteen of the last fourteen years you remembered my birthday! That's wonderful!"

What if we tried shifting our focus? What if we spent time during our team meetings to explore things that were *successful*? By fully understanding our successes, we ensure that we repeat them in other areas of our applications.

For example, if we learned that a particular design layout encouraged more purchases on a retail website, how could we apply that knowledge to increase reservations on a hotel website? Are there parallels that we can take advantage of? If so, what are they?

What if we were getting positive feedback on a change we recently made to a commenting engine on our website? If we only read them briefly, smiled, and went back to fixing bugs, we might miss opportunities to explore what's working for our users.

Again, I'm not encouraging you to be pie-in-the-sky optimists who only listen to positive feedback, but I think a case can be made that positive feedback provides equal amounts of insight as negative feedback.

Additionally, when you take time to focus on exploring things that work, you're not only reminded of your successes, but you open yourself to new insights. A mind filled with positivity simply works better.

We also need to be mindful of the negativity that *we* bring to the experience. I've sat in on discussions with developers as they complain about the proverbial stupid user. The application's design is never the problem. It's always the user's fault, and we blame them:

"They're just lazy."

"No matter how easy you make it, they'll never use it."

I've fallen victim to this sort of thinking myself. It's easy to do.

Lee Ross, a Stanford psychologist, defines this as the *Fundamental Attribution Error*:

> Essentially, the error lies in our inclination to attribute people's behavior to *the way they are* rather than *the situation they are in.*

Fundamental Attribution Error can adversely affect the way we relate to our users. It blinds us to what we're doing wrong.

For example, let's say we're frustrated because our users continually forget to properly log out of our in-house corporate filing system. We've educated them numerous times on the importance of logging out and we've even tried moving the logout button to various locations on the screen to increase visibility. However, users continually leave their session open, creating problems when they try to log in from another location.

In this case, it might be easy to blame users for not clicking the clearly visible logout button. We might even try threatening disciplinary action for failing to comply with logout procedures. Of course, this is the wrong frame of mind. It's obvious that the system is failing the user, not the other way around.

So we might have to go explore what's preventing users from logging out correctly. Perhaps it doesn't have to do with our application at all. When we visit and observe our users, we realize that their workflow is really not conducive to remembering to log out.

We discover that users walk away from their computer with the intention of returning but get sidetracked and don't return for several minutes or even hours.

After this realization, we decide to create an auto-logout function that activates after 30 minutes of inactivity.

This is what user-centered design helps us do. Every user behavior (whether positive or negative) is a reaction to our application. It's our job to learn why our users are reacting the way they are. The Fundamental Attribution Error works against this by introducing negative assumptions about our users and clouding our perceptions of what's really happening.

Creating amazing software experiences requires a great deal of self-motivation. You have to possess a deep desire to get things right. Do your best to eliminate negative language and attitudes. This will help you and your team remain positive, focused, and moving forward.

The Short Version

- Although working with users can be difficult, they're invaluable assets in creating a successful software application.
- Users aren't always right. Oftentimes, they're terrible at describing or understanding what they need. It's our job to continually ask questions and get to the root of what they're asking for.
- Bring users into your development process and educate them on using the right terminology. Give them the tools to better explain their needs.
- Users have their own way of approaching problems. Learn how to work with different personalities so you can get the most from your users.
- Work hard to remove negative language and attitudes. Avoid the Fundamental Attribution Error, which is "the inclination to explain people's behavior *by the way they are* rather than *the situation they are in.*"

CHAPTER 4

Having a Plan

"Goals are dreams with deadlines."

—Diana Scharf Hunt

When our team began to implement user-centered design practices at the hospital, it became apparent that we needed a plan. We couldn't say we were going to start putting users first and then just go about our business. We needed to have documentation, from beginning to end, that would help us complete the entire process correctly.

We also needed to communicate our vision for what we were trying to achieve. Not just to the hospital but to ourselves: What was our purpose? Overall, what did we want to achieve as a team? How did we provide value to our users and the organization?

We decided that a template was needed to help us fill in the blanks and effectively walk through the user-centered design process.

Building line-of-business applications for an organization requires that you wear many hats. One minute you're building an application to help the human resources department manage their employees and the next you're developing something to assist the finance department with their invoices. By having a template to revisit, our team is able to keep all of our projects headed in the same direction.

For the nonenterprise developer, it's equally important to have a plan in place before you start writing code. You should also spend time thinking about what you're trying to achieve with your applications, even if you're building them just for fun.

Essentially, having and documenting a strategic plan ensures that you're creating applications in a standardized pattern. A plan protects you from forgetting important features or user requests.

For our team we have a documented process that starts with planning, moves to implementation and testing, and finalizes with deployment and maintenance.

When working on a team, this is vital, because at some point, you may be asked to help colleagues with their project. If they're using the same standardized process to develop their application, it's easier for you to review their documentation and immediately get started.

Our template has the following core components:

- Team mission statement
- Project details
- User requirements
- Functional requirements
- Database/dataflow diagrams
- Screenshots of prototypes

At the hospital we use the template to educate users about our process. They know that when working with a member of our team, there's a standardized way in which we complete our projects. The more our users have worked within this structure, the more familiar they've become with what's needed to complete an application. Effectively, the template helps us help them and vice versa!

There are several industry terms for this type of documentation. Our template is part of an overall Software Development Life Cycle; some firms call theirs a Request for Proposal or Letter of Intent. The specifics of these documents are outside the scope of our discussion. However, I would encourage you to look at how other software development teams document their process.

How Do I Know Which Plan Is Right for Me?

I understand that the template I'm proposing may not fit your work environment or project. That's OK. What I want you to understand is that having a plan in place before you start writing code is a great way to ensure success.

I liken it to painting a room. If you're doing it right, you don't just walk in and start slathering paint all over the walls.

Let's think about all the steps involved in planning to paint your living room:

1. Measure the room to get a sense of how big the space is and how much paint you'll need.
2. Look at the furniture and lighting fixtures, and estimate how much natural light enters the room.
3. Go to the hardware store and look through many color swatches. Talk to the store clerk and ask about the different qualities of each brand.

4. Bring home a sample color and apply it to a small section of a wall. Wait for it to dry and make sure it's the color you want.

5. Clean all the walls, tape the edges, fix any small holes and defects, and apply a priming coat.

All of this comes before you start the official project of painting the living room. Imagine if you applied this same type of commitment to your software projects before writing code. What if you spent most of your time researching the problem space and asking users about their needs? What if you explored the problem by building prototypes and quick mock-ups or screenshots?

My presumption is that you would spend less time writing unnecessary code or building features no one needs. That's why having a plan should be a crucial part of your user-centered design process. It's more than just collecting feedback from users; it's stepping through a strategic process to make sure you've covered all your bases.

However, I'm not suggesting that it's as simple as completing a plan and going off to write the code. Using our metaphor, building an application is like painting a room that changes its shape every day. With user-centered design, we continually gain new insights. Some of these insights are so significant that they change the course of development.

Software development is a dynamic process; it's impossible to prescribe a specific workflow. Practicing user-centered design means you'll be reacting to discoveries that were not included in your original plan. The software design team at EffectiveUI has a great way of looking at it:

> No matter how well you think you understand the domain and no matter how earnestly you've thought through the requirements, there is still great uncertainty in the original facts and premises and a vast depth of the unknown still awaiting you. As with battle, the outcome will be determined at least as much by what comes during the course of the project as by what comes before it.

With that said, it doesn't mean we shouldn't keep a template or framework for the steps we intend to take. At the very least, you should be creating some form of roadmap so that you're executing your user-centered design process in a meaningful way.

Creating a Team Mission Statement

A team mission statement is a great way to set the tone of your template. Without having an understanding of what your team is trying to achieve, how can you proceed forward with any project? A mission statement has the power to remind the team of its purpose. Additionally, it gives you a fundamental understanding of the work you're trying to complete. You can revisit your mission statement when making difficult decisions on a project.

We decided our team mission statement should be different from our organization's mission statement. It's not that we disagreed with the mission of the hospital, but we needed something more specific for what our team was trying to achieve. Therefore, we examined the organization's mission statement and customized it to better reflect our team's purpose. We decided our team was responsible for:

> Developing simple innovative solutions to empower users in achieving the highest standards in patient care and service

The hospital's mission is to provide the highest standards in patient care and service. The mission for our team is to provide simple and innovative solutions so they can achieve that.

Using this mission statement while evaluating our applications, we ask ourselves:

- Is this application simple and easy to use?
- Is this application innovative? Can we implement newer technology that makes it even better?
- Is this application an impediment, or is it empowering staff to provide the best care for our patients?

Our project template has the team's mission statement at the very beginning. It's a reminder of the team's commitment to the hospital and one another. If you work on a team in an organization of any size, consider what your mission statement might be.

Defining Your Project

In order to begin heading in the right direction, you have to be able to summarize what you're trying to achieve with your application: What's the point? Why are you building it? Who will the application serve? How will it provide value?

It seems obvious that your project should be able to answer these questions, but I find it valuable to take the time to document this information. The act of documenting what you want to accomplish can help you better understand your users' needs. I also use this process as a point for users to give me feedback. Something as simple as the title of the project can have a dramatic effect on its outcome. An example of this was a project I worked on for our Rapid Response Team (RRT).

The RRT urgently responds to patients when their vitals (heart rate, respiratory rate, blood pressure, etc.) are in a "danger zone." If an RRT nurse can respond before the situation becomes critical, he can provide proactive care and save a patient's life, as well as increase his chances for a successful clinical outcome.

After the first few rounds of meetings with staff, I decided I was going to provide a database solution for RRT nurses to document their process. By collecting information about what happens during an RRT situation, we could look for ways to improve the process and help nurses respond in a timely manner.

I titled the project Rapid Response Team Database.

The lead physician involved with the project saw the title and asked me a question:

> "Why are you calling this the Rapid Response Team Database?"
>
> "Well," I replied, "a database will allow the team to document their process. With this data, we can produce reports and look for ways to make response times faster."
>
> "That's great," he said, "however, I'm having a problem with that. This project should include more than just the Rapid Response Team. Really, it should be called the Rapid Response System. You see, in order for us to respond effectively, we need a system that involves all patient care providers, not just the Rapid Response Team. That's how we'll make a big difference."

Correcting the title of the project uncovered a big insight. I realized that, in order for me to meet the needs of users (and hopefully save patients' lives), I needed to expand the scope of the project to include members outside the RRT. I needed to start thinking of the project as an entire system, rather than just a small database for one specific team.

If I hadn't taken the time to describe my understanding of the project's goals, I would've grossly miscalculated when I began development. I would've created an application that was too small in scope, reducing the impact.

In this case, the title made a huge difference in my understanding of the project.

Our project template has a section "Project Details" on page 116 that includes these subsections:

- Title
- Description
- List of Stakeholders
- Impact Assessment

The project title and description should reflect the entire scope of the project. While the title gives you a convenient way to refer to the project, the description should summarize what the project will achieve.

The section on stakeholders may or may not be necessary for your situation. If you were delivering an application to a specific group of people, then I would advise you to include a list of individuals who will share the responsibility of the project with you. If your project is for the mass market, you might consider revising this section to be "Potential

Users." Essentially, you should take a moment to consider the types of users you want to have an impact on.

If you do have stakeholders, then their job is to provide you with the information you need so you can create a successful application. By listing key stakeholders, you know whom you can count on when you have a question or need clarification. This helps everyone understand who's involved in the user-centered design process.

Finally, the impact assessment describes the impact the application will make on the environment in which it will be deployed. In other words, the assessment should summarize whom or what will be affected as a result of the application (both positively and negatively). This is a great way to help keep your eyes on the prize.

Again, this may not work for your situation. In an enterprise development role, it's always a good idea to consider how your application will impact the organization. This will help your team prioritize projects.

If you're working on your own, you might consider the personal impact of the project: What do you hope to gain from working on this application? How will this project help you in advancing your craft? What would you like to gain from your work?

You might also consider reviewing the impact assessment after each project is completed. This way you can see if the application had the impact you were looking for. If possible, consider having users review the impact assessment before you start the project to make sure your vision matches theirs.

Collecting User Requirements

Collecting user requirements is the most important part of your user-centered strategy. The user requirements set the foundation for the remaining steps in the user-centered design process. Without properly defined user requirements, it's impossible to move forward in the right direction.

The process of collecting user requirements demands that you take users' abstract requests and convert them into meaningful needs. Documenting these needs requires you to summarize what's needed. By showing requirements to your users, you can ensure you've correctly understood their needs.

There's something powerful about showing users their requests in writing. Many times, I've been corrected when I show them my summarized list of their requirements. They'll say, "Yeah, I see how you thought that's what I needed, but actually I need something different." Documenting user requirements has saved me countless hours of wasted development time and heartache.

To be clear, user requirements are not technical. In fact, this part of your Software Development Life Cycle (SDLC) should avoid technological solutions. User requirements are the users' needs, not a specification sheet of what you're going to deliver.

Collecting user requirements is so vital to a successful project that I often refuse to write a line of code until I've had several meetings with users to flesh out their requirements. Without proper communication and understanding between the developer and the user, it's impossible to create an effective application. Documenting user requirements is the best way to encourage that kind of communication.

If you were not working with a direct client or user, then I would advise taking time to consider what potential users would require from your application. Coworkers, family, and friends can be a great resource for this. Consider showing them your requirements and get feedback on whether your user requirements match theirs.

During graduate school I worked on a proof-of-concept iPhone application for organizing potlucks. One of the first steps the team took was to brainstorm all the user requirements for planning a potluck. Things like contacting friends, organizing a list of meals, and keeping party attendees updated on the latest developments were requirements that began to surface. After our brainstorming concluded, I felt like we had the space pretty well covered.

However, when we went out and talked to our family and friends, we learned of several new requirements that we hadn't considered. The fact was that I planned potlucks much differently than some of my friends. The things that I cared about weren't as important to them and vice versa.

If you've spent months developing a project only to discover you built something your users didn't need, it's time to consider collecting and documenting user requirements.

Creating Functional Requirements

You may be confused about the difference between user and functional requirements. A user requirement is what the user needs; a functional requirement is what the application needs. Essentially, functional requirements can be seen as the technical specifications of the project. These are the individual functions you plan to deliver through your application to meet the user's request.

Our potluck application had a variety of user requirements for planning potluck parties. While collecting user requirements, it was difficult to remain focused on discussing requirements and not get sidetracked by trying to find solutions. We remained focused on understanding what users needed to plan a successful gathering. When we reached the stage of discussing functional requirements, we could finally brainstorm on how we might meet those needs with our application.

For instance, we observed that a consistent user requirement for planning a potluck was to have attendees notified when something had changed. For example, an attendee may change his mind and decide to bring a dessert instead of a side dish. If two other people were planning to bring desert, it would be important to let him know so he could consider revising his choice. It was also important for attendees to know who was planning on attending the event. They wanted to be notified if someone cancelled or did not plan on attending.

The team reviewed several technical solutions. We also reviewed other applications and how they dealt with similar situations. We asked users what technologies they were currently using to meet their needs and asked about the pros and cons of those services.

Eventually, we decided that iOS notifications were the best way to respond to users' needs. Therefore, we ended up listing the ability for the application to send iOS notifications as a functional requirement, as shown in Figure 4-1.

In your template, consider connecting each functional requirement to the user requirement it meets.

At the hospital our template includes columns so we can number our user and functional requirements. This allows us to make connections between them. You might have one user requirement and several functional requirements that meet that need. By having these lists numbered, it makes it easy to quickly review them and make sure we've connected a functional requirement to each user requirement.

If you're working for a specific group of users or client, then the list of functional requirements can help you communicate to users how your development process works. When they see their user requirements translated into a list of technological solutions, it becomes an effective tool for explaining your role in the process.

Figure 4-1. Potluck application sending an iOS notification to notify party attendees that a new attendee accepted the party invitation

I find that this also helps with users who make last-minute requests. If a user changes his mind about what he needs, then the process has to start over. You'll have to document his new request and convert it to a functional requirement. You can use this process to explain why extra time is required in adding the new request to the project. On more than one occasion, I've had users decide against adding a new feature once they saw how it affected the delivery of other functional requirements.

Documenting Data and Workflow Models

If the application you're building relies on a dataset or multiple datasets, it's a good idea to include diagrams of how that data is structured, retrieved, and transferred. Tools, like Microsoft Visio, provide templates for creating database and dataflow diagrams.

A *database diagram* depicting the structure and organization of your database can be a helpful tool. It allows you to see what data elements are available and how you might access them. I often keep a printed version of my database diagram at my desk. I realize this process is a bit analog, but I find it easier than hunting through my database software to look for a particular field. Obviously, if you have an extremely large database, printing a diagram of it would not be an option. If this is the case, you might consider a modified diagram that focuses on the elements you plan to use in your application.

Another helpful tool is the *workflow diagram* or *dataflow diagram*. I use workflow diagrams for projects that have a complex series of steps to complete an action or where multiple people are involved to achieve an outcome. Workflow diagrams allow you to consider all the steps required for a user or group of users to complete an action.

It can require some time to create this, but the diagram will free you from having to manage the entire application's workflow from memory. Even something as simple as a vending machine can have several paths and conditions to consider, as depicted in Figure 4-2. It can be easy to miss a step or forget a critical path.

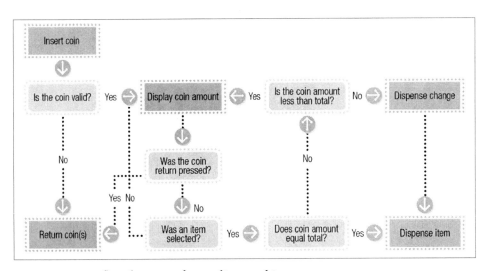

Figure 4-2. Dataflow diagram of a vending machine

The database and dataflow diagrams can be as simple or as complex as you want them to be. Obviously, the more detail the better, but I'd prefer a limited diagram to nothing at all.

Documenting Prototypes

Prototypes can be useful tools in assisting the user-centered design process. Prototypes allow you to translate the user and functional requirements into something tangible. How can users know what you intend to deliver if they can't see it?

I think the biggest challenge developers have with prototyping is that it takes away from the big reveal—that unmistakable high you get just before you show the user what you've been working on. In some ways this high is what keeps us motivated to continue developing our project in secrecy. If our motivation is to have a big unveiling, it causes us to hide our ideas from the user until we're finished.

In the book *Team Geek* (O'Reilly), authors Brian Fitzpatrick and Ben Collins-Sussman describe this problem perfectly:

> Deep down we all secretly wish to be geniuses. The ultimate geek fantasy is to be struck by an awesome new concept. You go into your Bat Cave for weeks or months, slaving away at a perfect implementation of your idea. You then "unleash" your software on the world, shocking everyone with your genius. Your peers are astonished by your cleverness. People line up to use your software. Fame and fortune follow naturally.

The problem with this approach is that if users haven't been included in the development process, then there's a greater chance they'll be disappointed when you're finished. The dramatic unveiling shouldn't motivate us. Instead, we should be driven by the desire to get things right, and the best way to do this is by having users involved throughout the entire process.

We'll talk more about prototyping in Chapter 8. For now, understand that your documentation should include screenshots and early mockups from your prototypes.

Reviewing Your Documentation

Another value of documenting the user-centered design process from the very beginning is you'll have the ability to review it long after the project has been completed. It can be an interesting and reflective exercise to see how your application changed over time. Reviewing old templates and documentation allows you to see the entire process, from conception to reality. It's a powerful tool to discover and gain insight into how your project changed over time.

Some of you may already have extensive contracts and specification sheets for your clients to sign. If you don't work in that type of environment, I encourage you to enforce stakeholders to sign a project plan, even if it feels a little awkward.

I've found that our users don't mind entering into this type of agreement. Most of them actually like to see a document that clearly states a plan to meet their needs—and they're willing to sign off on it. It makes them feel more like a client and not just a coworker.

In the enterprise development environment, I think that's how users should feel. Of course, our team doesn't consider this to be a legally binding document; it's just a simple way to elevate the importance of the documented plan.

In Appendix A, you'll find the project-planning template we use at the hospital. Feel free to use this as a guide to building your own. You may decide to rewrite our template to focus on other areas. That's fine.

At the end of the day, your plan should meet the needs of your team and users. As long you design it as a tool for documenting and following a standardized methodology, it should prove invaluable.

The Short Version

- Your team should have a mission statement that reflects your purpose and commitment to users and each other.
- Consider creating a project template that starts with planning, moves to implementation and testing, and ends with deployment and maintenance.
- You should include a project details section in your template. The project details should include the title of the project, a description of what it is, and an impact assessment, if appropriate.
- Your documented plan should include a list of user requirements. Essentially, this list represents your users' needs and should not include technological solutions.
- Functional requirements are a list of your application's needs. This list is focused on the technology and how it will meet each user requirement.
- If your application is reliant on a dataset or complex user workflow be sure to include database and/or dataflow diagrams in your documentation.
- Prototypes can be a powerful tool in the user-centered design process. Be sure to document any screenshots or early mockups of your prototype.
- Reviewing old documentation can be a valuable exercise in learning from previous mistakes.

CHAPTER 5

Creating a Personal Manifesto

> *"A goal is not always meant to be reached; it often*
> *serves simply as something to aim at."*
>
> —Bruce Lee

In the previous section, we talked about the importance of having a team mission statement. Having a clear vision, regardless if you're working on a team or developing software by yourself, is vital to being successful. After all, how can you possibly move in the right direction if you haven't decided what you ultimately want to achieve?

Robby Ingebretsen, a developer and co-creator of Pixel Lab, a user-experience design and software development studio, believes everyone should have a personal manifesto:

> I don't have a dictionary definition of manifesto at hand. I've avoided looking it up because I'm willing to hijack it (take that, word meanings!). I think of it this way: a manifesto is a declaration of why the thing you do makes the world better.

Ingebretsen believes developers should have a singular, overarching focus. It should be a summarized reason for why we're building software products.

In the previous chapter I discussed how our team builds applications to help our organization achieve "the highest standards of patient care and service." That's our team's singular focus. If we're not achieving that, then we're not delivering on our mission.

But here's another thing: not only should you have an overall mission statement, but you should also have a manifesto for each project you're working on.

For example, instead of saying, "I'm building a travel application," a manifesto would say, "I'm building an application that creates the experience and value of having a personal travel assistant."

Ingebretsen suggests that software development shop FiftyThree is a prime example of how great products come from having a clear manifesto.

FiftyThree, based in New York and Seattle, is responsible for the wildly successful iPad application Paper. Just two weeks after its release in the Apple App Store, Paper received over 1.5 million downloads, skyrocketing it to the top of the charts. The application, which allows you to paint, draw, and sketch, garnered critical praise, and in 2012 it won an Apple Design Award.

In a March 2012 interview with *The Verge*, Georg Petschnigg, co-founder of FiftyThree, talks about the mission of Paper:

> So Paper is—where ideas begin. Right? It's the place where you go to—like—sketch and write, draw, color, outline. It's—when you want to spend time with your ideas, Paper is the home for your ideas.

"Paper is the home for your ideas" sounds like a great manifesto to me. That's a singular vision. FiftyThree didn't set out to make another design tool or paint program. They built an application, displayed in Figure 5-1, which felt like the perfect home for your ideas. That's a specific manifesto with a clear vision in mind.

Figure 5-1. Paper for the iPad, by FiftyThree

When you approach your applications with a manifesto like FiftyThree did with Paper, it begins to shape your path and direction. It helps you know what features you want to include, and more importantly, what features you'll leave out. By constantly comparing your progress against your vision statement, you ensure that you're headed in the right direction. This leads me to my next point.

Exercising Restraint

A mistake that I see developers make time and again, myself included, is many of us allow our applications to become bloated with features. To me, when I see an application with too many features, many of which I don't want or need, it's clear to me that the developers lacked a manifesto or vision. They put technology first and became hyper-focused on what they could do and not what they should do.

I think the reason we do this is because, by our very nature, we love technology. We want to showcase it. To us, the value of our applications comes from what it can do.

When developers show off their work, what do they often focus on? They talk about the features, which showcase the elements they're most proud of and the technological hurdles they were able to surpass.

I don't think there's anything wrong with being proud of our programming skills; however, we need to remember that they are of little value to users if we're not giving them what they need.

For example, if we were making an instant messaging application, we might be excited that we've implemented GPS location technology, allowing users to see where their messages are coming from. However, if it's a chore to send messages to a fellow user, how valuable is our application overall? Users may be impressed by the GPS location feature, but because the application fails at meeting their core needs, they'll decide not to use it.

The phrase, "less is more" may come to mind.

In my experience, many developers struggle with this concept. It's not that they don't want their applications to be easy to use—it's just difficult to decide what features are paramount to the experience. Developers often struggle with layout, organization, and prioritization of features. They make the mistake of hiding valuable features their users want in order to promote functionality they're proud of.

Bill Buxton, principal researcher at Microsoft Research, has a primary axiom:

> Everything is best for something and worst for something else. The trick is knowing what is what, for what, when, for whom, where, and most importantly, why.

This is why we must have a manifesto or some form of vision statement for our applications. As developers, we need a singular vision to return to when our development gets mired in features and technical roadblocks. We need to be reminded of what we're ultimately trying to achieve.

One way to create a manifesto is by having a story to tell and knowing that narrative well.

Building a Narrative

FiftyThree wanted Paper to be an application that allowed users to capture their ideas. They wanted it to have broad appeal and not be limited to just professional artists. They believed that when people used Paper their ideas should flourish, not be encumbered by limitations or complex tool sets.

To achieve this, FiftyThree needed a story that aligned with their manifesto. They needed to clearly understand how Paper could accomplish what it was designed to achieve. The developers and designers had to evaluate features and functionality to make sure they made sense within the context of Paper's story.

An application's narrative is an ongoing story of how the application shapes the lives of its users. Manifestos are a specific and declarative statement, whereas narratives can be rich with detailed scenarios of how the application will be used.

Julian Walker, the lead engineer behind Paper, says that FiftyThree didn't implement a specific product development technique. Instead, they relied on their story for Paper:

> At Fifty Three, we don't have any hifalutin ideas on product development—we're not out there professing any techniques, but what we started calling our process was "narrative-based design."
>
> Developers always tend to want to give the user more power, especially if they can—easily. They're like: "The feature's almost built. All we have to do is add the button!" And that may not always fit into the story.

When you use Paper, you can see that FiftyThree's story did not include having a lot of features. Julian is a brilliant engineer, and I have no doubt that he could've built a complex design tool. But complex features didn't align with FiftyThree's vision. They felt out of place within Paper's narrative and manifesto.

Paper has only six tools and a limited set of default color choices, which is completely intentional. By exploring the act of generating ideas with drawing and painting, FiftyThree realized that other applications reduced creativity by overloading users with features. Paper has since been updated to include a color mixer, but it's still clear that FiftyThree approaches each additional feature with restraint.

Paper's narrative encourages simplicity by enforcing reduction. When using Paper, you become focused on what you want to draw, not how you want to draw it. This reduction in complexity allows users to focus on their creativity, and this is the key to Paper's success.

For example, let's say I'm working on a line of t-shirts for a promotional giveaway. As I begin to sketch, Paper's design—or narrative—keeps me focused on the overall concept of my idea. For instance, if I'm making one of the shirts red, Paper provides only one shade of red to choose from. I pick that color and I move on.

Other design tools would present me with a color picker and virtually limitless color options. When I'm given that many choices, I begin to focus on picking the perfect color of red. That's not to say having options is a bad thing (eventually FiftyThree did add the ability to mix colors); however, it works against FiftyThree's manifesto. They want me to stay focused on my idea for the t-shirt design, not picking the perfect color.

As it turns out, FiftyThree's narrative-based design works very well and, as a result, I'm much more creative when using Paper. By reducing color choices and providing limited but highly stylized tools, Paper is unlike any other application I use for my creative needs. Therefore, it's become my default tool for exploring ideas and early concepts.

Just as Petschnigg described, Paper has become the home for my ideas.

Consider the story of your application: What elements should it include? What elements should be left out? Are the features you've provided following the story you were trying to tell?

Creating Personas

One way you can augment your narrative is by creating a persona.

A persona is a character-driven element that helps you remember who you're building the application for. It's a fictional character that is a personification of your real users. To create a persona, you should be asking your users questions like:

- Name one of your favorite products. Why is it better than other similar products?

- What product frustrates you the most? Why? What would you do to improve it?

- If you could create the perfect application to help you with this task, what would it look like? What would it do?

By asking questions like these, you'll gain a better understanding of what motivates your users and what experiences they enjoy. For example, listening to a user describe features they love about their music player may provide insight into a sports application you're building. At first, it may appear that these two products are unrelated. However, if you're willing to listen, it's possible that you'll learn new ways to improve the user experience in your own applications.

With the information you collect from your users, you'll craft a persona. It should include details like:

- Name
- Age
- Marital and family status
- Location
- Occupation
- Hobbies and favorite items
- Needs and frustrations

It can also include pictures of what you imagine the person looks like and any other information that brings the persona to life. In Appendix A you'll find an example persona for a user of Paper for the iPad.

The persona can prove vitally important in situations where you have distance between you and the user. An example might be if you're creating something for the mass market, like a smartphone application. If you're not working directly with users, the persona will describe the type of people using your application. If necessary, talk with prospective users and create a persona from your findings. You might even use them to create your persona directly (removing their personal information, of course).

A persona is a highly reflective instrument that helps you consider all aspects of a user. With it you can dive deep into their psyche and imagine what motivates them. You spend time articulating their frustrations and what makes them happy.

When the persona is rooted in the information you've collected from users, it can have a very tangible effect.

Creating Scenarios

Once you have personas to reflect the users of your application, you can begin the process of creating scenarios. Scenarios are mini stories that reflect situations your personas may find themselves in. In a scenario, you pay particular attention to how your application will enhance the experience of the user.

The more detail you have in your personas, the easier it is for you to imagine how they will react to a given scenario. As its name implies, scenarios are like scenes in a movie. The persona is the character, and your application can be seen as the plot device, or a way to advance the story.

Ideally you'll create many scenarios and situations that your persona will encounter with your application. If you're honest about your application's limitations, exploring different scenarios can help you understand just how much of an issue a particular limitation is.

For instance, let's say we're building a smartphone application that helps Susan, our persona, find low-fat recipes. Here would be some appropriate scenarios we might encounter:

- Susan is at home. She's looking through her cupboards and trying to locate items for a chosen recipe. How might our application help with that?
- Susan is at the park with her children. She wants to find a lasagna recipe to cook for dinner. What features of the application would she use to accomplish this?
- Susan is talking on her smartphone with a friend about a recipe for a low-fat casserole. How might she send this recipe to her friend? Could she accomplish this without hanging up the phone?
- Susan is out shopping and wants to locate a particular spice that's used in a recipe she's found. How would the application assist her in finding it?

Scenarios can be as detailed as needed in order to envision how your application will respond. Additionally, when you combine these scenarios with the rich personalities of your personas, you can evaluate your design decisions and decide if they meet your users' needs.

As a part of the user-centered design process, you should take time to consider your narrative, personas, and scenarios: each of these will help you create a clear path to your goal. It can also help you realize when you've strayed from your vision and added unnecessary features. If possible, let users review your personas and scenarios and allow them to give you feedback.

The combination of a manifesto and a detailed narrative with personas and scenarios can shape the path and direction of your software development.

The Short Version

- Consider having a manifesto or vision statement for your application. A manifesto is the overall purpose and vision for your application.

- By building a narrative, you take the declarative statement of your manifesto and weave a rich story of how your application can be used.

- Personas are fictional, character-driven elements that personify your ideal user. Use personas to enhance your narrative and help tell the story of your application.

- Scenarios, just like scenes in a movie, are specific situations your personas might find themselves in. Using scenarios, you can explore how the application will respond (or not respond) to the user's needs.

CHAPTER 6
Creativity and User Experience

"Good artists borrow, great artists steal."
—Pablo Picasso

At this point, it's worth noting that FiftyThree's artistic sensibilities can be a bit intimidating. I have no problem admitting that part of Paper's success is attributed to their team's natural design intuitions.

The example of FiftyThree isn't, "Look! If you're using user-centered design you can build amazingly beautiful applications, too!" The point is that we should admire Fifty-Three's execution of their vision. In the iPad marketplace, there are plenty of applications that let users draw and paint. FiftyThree could have created an uninspired application with all the same feature sets and complexity.

Instead, they decided to re-examine how their competitors' applications might be stifling creativity and came up with a unique vision for Paper. More importantly, they used this vision to create a narrative that helped them stay focused on their mission. That is the lesson we learn from them.

How would your application (and, frankly, anything else you might be working on) be different if you enforced this same level of dedication?

The previous chapter is an example of focus, not creativity. Creativity cannot help you if you don't have a vision or narrative for your application. We see this in applications that are full of creative intentions but miss their core functionality and purpose. These applications may be beautiful to look at, but they are virtually useless to us.

Are there people who are naturally more creative? Absolutely. However, I've heard many developers say things like, "I'm not creative" or "I'm not an artist, so my user interface (UI) is going to be basic." I'm disheartened when I hear things like that. There's no need to accept grayscale graphics or Comic Sans font as a way of life. We shouldn't be creating applications that are uninspired and thoughtless. If we're willing to work a little harder, we can all do better.

Our users are becoming a savvy and demanding bunch. Gone are the days of just being happy with decreased load times or added features. Users expect a rich experience. They expect applications to be thoughtfully designed and engaging.

Today, there are services like on-demand movie rentals, digital video recorders (DVRs), checkout kiosks, and online banking. People are using these applications and becoming far more discerning about what they want and don't want.

We have to adapt. We have to accept that it's not all about functionality.

You can find hundreds of applications that help you complete a particular task, but only a few will make completing that task delightful.

Now, don't misunderstand me. Applications will always rise and fall based on their functionality. If an application provides no value or does not function as it was designed, you're sunk. There is no amount of magical glaze or fancy UI to fix poor functionality. However, we have to concede that aesthetics and design are a huge part of the user experience. Many of us don't have access to a team of designers, so we need to spend time exploring our own creativity in order to achieve our application's user experience goals.

Having User-Experience Goals

User-centered design is more than collecting user requirements and converting them to functional requirements. You should also consider what kind of experience the user will have while completing tasks. By taking the time and defining user-experience goals, we can ensure that our application creates an experience that meets users' expectations.

The difference between user requirements and user-experience goals might be confusing. After all, shouldn't it be a requirement that users have a great experience with our application? Of course that's true; however, it's better to have specific goals in mind. For instance, we might consider some of the following questions:

- How important is load time? Will the user be willing to wait for things to load if it means we can provide a richer experience?
- How will users be interacting with the application? Will they use touch, voice, gestures, keyboard and mouse, or a combination of these things? How would the type of input affect the way I present information to them?
- Should the application be fun to use? Do I want users to be amused and surprised or do they expect something consistent?

- What tone of language should I use to communicate with the user? Is it whimsical, professional, supportive, or energetic? Is the language I've chosen consistent throughout the application?

When users approach an application, they're expecting a specific kind of experience. A children's learning site would feel sterile and distant if it used professional language. However, if a banking site were full of whimsy and bright primary colors, users would think twice about leaving their money there.

That's not to say that you can't be creative and test conventional wisdom. A bank, for instance, could dedicate a section of its website to teaching kids about the importance of saving money. Let's consider some of the user-experience goals for a project like this:

- Design should include bright colors and feature the bank's new mascot, "Scotty the Wise Owl."
- Language should be written at a second-grade level. Avoid industry jargon and banking terminology.
- Games should be available to support the message that saving money is cool and exciting.
- Animations and videos should be provided to keep children entertained and engaged.
- Include activities that can be printed and shared with the family offline.

If you're not thinking about the experience your users are expecting, you may be out of step and confusing them. Taking the time to list your user-experience goals will help you create a consistent experience throughout your application. This may require being creative, and most developers, being of the dominant left-brained ilk, struggle with these types of tasks. Let's explore ways we can encourage ourselves to think more creatively.

Creativity Requires Courage and Hard Work

I think some developers believe that design and creativity are frivolous. They believe it's all just fluff and the real meat of an application is in its code. They're wrong. The reality is that creativity requires a significant amount of personal resolve and grit.

It also requires courage, especially if you're not used to expressing yourself creatively. You have to be vulnerable, try different things, and be OK with being uncomfortable.

I deeply admire developers who are courageous in their creativity, those who take risks and challenge conventional wisdom regardless if they're successful or not. Being creative takes real guts. Uncertainty, courage, and creativity are where innovation grows; and while the ground may be fertile, it requires determination for anything to take root.

Most artists agree that creativity comes from practice, dedication, and plain old hard work.

In Debbie Millman's book, *How to Think Like a Great Graphic Designer* (Allworth Press), world-famous graphic designer Milton Glasser tells the author what has led to his nearly 50 years of creative success:

> I don't know. Just staying at the desk and turning out the work and trying to do it as well as I can. I am also a very persistent man: a stubborn, persistent man. And the reward is still the same reward: doing things that have quality, that are still powerful, and that reach people. And, of course, the sheer joy of doing it. I love coming in to my office and working.

Creativity requires the relentless pursuit of the perfect design. You have to be prepared to fail and try again. It's more than just having a great idea—it's the delivery of that idea. You have to be willing to bring your creativity into the sunlight so it can be harshly examined. Only then will you be able to discover great ideas and discard the rest. In his book *Untitled: Thoughts on the Creative Process* (Creative Collective), author Blaine Hogan details what's required of us to push the boundaries of our creativity:

> Your vision casting must be in direct proportion to the work you are willing to do to make your vision come to life.
>
> I know a lot of people with a lot of really great ideas but only a few who actually end up making things. And I know even far fewer who end up creating great work.
>
> Talent is rarely the issue, if you're wondering.
>
> No, the real issue is whether or not we're willing to risk our reputations to do the painful work required to create great things, or take the easy way out by underselling our pitches, regurgitating old visions, and recreating what we know.

There's no reason to wish that you were more creative. Be willing to do the hard work necessary in gaining the creative insight you desire.

Pick Up a Pencil

One way to exercise your creativity is to spend time sketching your ideas. I know many recoil at the thought of drawing, but I assure you it has many benefits.

First of all, when we sketch, we're using the right side of our brains, the part responsible for abstract thinking and intuition. Programming, on the other hand, is very much a left-brained activity. And while the left side of our brain is great for analytical and logical reasoning (e.g., writing code), it's got a poor track record for discovering abstract patterns and new insights. Concepts that are difficult to express in code or logical reasoning might simply appear when you try to draw them. Yet so many developers avoid expressing their ideas this way, believing they must be artistic in order to use the tools of an artist. However, just because you can't draw the *Mona Lisa*, it doesn't mean that drawing can't help you.

At the Agile UX New York City 2012 conference, Jeff Gothelf presented "Demystifying Design: Fewer secrets, bigger impacts." In his presentation, he explained that if you could draw a triangle, square, or circle, you could draw just about any user interface. I agree. Unlike code, drawing requires a smaller investment of time and offers the agility to quickly communicate ideas. There's virtually no commitment. If an idea isn't working, you can throw it out and start drawing something else. You tell me what's easier to throw away: a five-minute sketch of some basic shapes or a five-hour coding example? I rest my case.

One of the most valuable tools I have in my office is my dry-erase board. During meetings, it's not uncommon for me to use the board to visually communicate all sorts of ideas. Sometimes, I'll use it to simply write down words I hear when a user is talking. Not only does this reinforce to them that I'm actively listening, but they're also able to see what I'm parsing out as a result of our discussion. The application begins to take shape just by isolating words alone.

I can also use the dry-erase board to draw an early layout of the interface. I do this, as you can see in Figure 6-1, by drawing squares, lines and other basic shapes, so the user can see how I'm interpreting what they're telling me. Many times, by drawing early sketches, I can discover areas where I've completely misunderstood what the user was describing; this has saved me countless hours of programming things the user didn't want.

Once, I had a user so exasperated by my inability understand that she took the pen from me and started drawing. It took only minutes before I finally understood what she was trying to say. At the very least, you should consider having tools like pens, paper, or dry-erase boards available. Again, people have many different ways of analyzing and describing a problem. You may not prefer to draw, but it might be the perfect tool for one of your users to communicate. Explore those possibilities with your users and you might save yourself time and frustration.

A core component of the user-centered design process is exploring effective ways to communicate with users. Be willing to try new things if your meetings are falling flat and you're leaving confused. If your users aren't giving you what you need, try other methods. Drawing can be fun and it might spark less-enthused users into participating.

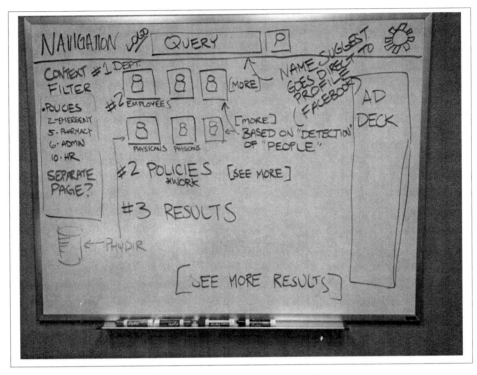

Figure 6-1. One of the many drawings from my dry-erase board

Creative Freedom

Let's face it: sometimes working on the same project day in and day out can be a drain. Sitting at your desk, confronted with the same problems you had yesterday and the day before can obliterate your motivation. Make sure you're spending time outside your current projects to exercise your creative muscles and continue growing new ideas.

Consider this: perhaps you can work on a project that has nothing to do with what you're currently working on. It might not even be a software program. Maybe it's woodworking, painting, or making music. If that's too creative, try exploring new technologies or coding frameworks. Perhaps you could build an application with a web service you've never used before like Twitter, Facebook, Flickr, Yahoo! Weather, etc.

Daniel Pink, author of *Drive: The Surprising Truth About What Motivates Us* (Riverhead Books), shares the story of how one company dedicates an entire day each quarter to creative freedom. The company is called Atlassian and its cofounder Mike Cannon-Brookes has come up with what he calls "ShipIt Days" (they used to be referred to as "FedEx Days" but have since been renamed due to copyright infringement). Atlassian's ShipIt Days allow software engineers a free day to work on whatever they want with whomever they want. The only requirement is that engineers must ship their work to their colleagues the next day, hence the name.

Pink explains how ShipIt Days work:

> At two P.M. on a Thursday, the day begins. Engineers, including Cannon-Brookes himself, crash out new code or an elegant hack—any way they want, with anyone they want. Many work through the night. Then, at four P.M. on Friday, they show the results to the rest of the company in a wild-and-woolly all-hands meeting stocked with ample quantities of cold beer and chocolate cake. Atlassian calls these twenty-four hour bursts of freedom and creativity ["ShipIt Days"]—because people have to deliver something overnight. And deliver Atlassians have. Over the years, this odd little exercise has produced an array of software fixes that might otherwise never have emerged.

Imagine if you and your team could take a day out each quarter—or month—and focus on whatever you wanted. Atlassian realizes the value in this creative freedom and is willing to put its money where its mouth is. I'm sure many engineers come back the next day with ideas or demonstrations that have very little immediate value. But that's not the point. Atlassian wants to encourage a company culture that embraces freedom to explore new ideas and celebrates out-of-the-box thinking.

If you're working in an enterprise environment or software development shop, consider showing your boss supportive articles about the power of creative freedom. Suggest that your company should implement ShipIt Days. Be willing to organize it and educate others about how it will work. It could be the very thing your company needs to spark innovation and re-engage its employees.

If you're on your own, make sure you're setting aside time to explore creative outlets. Go to the park and take your camera. Produce a movie with your kids and show it to the family with a big premiere. Create an Instagram account and take pictures of interesting things you encounter.

It really doesn't matter how you choose to express yourself creatively, as long as you're being purposeful and making time to do it.

Understanding Your Goal

As I stated in the previous chapter, a clear vision and goal for your project is paramount to its success. Understanding your goal has implications for creative exploration as well. You see, when you truly understand what you're setting out to achieve, it can be easier to push aside naysayers. That can be important when you're in the vulnerable stages of early creativity.

Jeff Weir is a UX designer for Microsoft, and his project Viscosity is a great example of understanding your goal.

Viscosity is an award-winning, web-based application that allows users to spread multi-colored paint into masterpieces. Ultimately, it's a digital representation of the viscous nature of paint, as shown in Figure 6-2. Users have created and shared thousands of art projects using Viscosity. They're also able to see an ever-expanding slideshow of one another's creative works.

When evaluating Weir's work on Viscosity, one might deem it to be superfluous. A web application that allows users to spread paint around—what's the point?

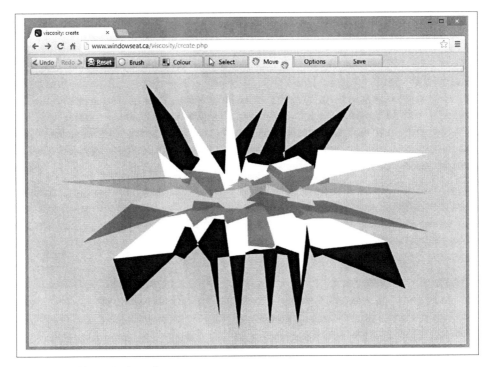

Figure 6-2. Viscosity interface

Weir doesn't really see a need for a point:

> I had a lot of people telling me why I should stop. What's the point? How are you even going to make money at this? And none of those were goals for me. The goal wasn't to make money—the goal was to make something awesome.

This isn't to suggest that one must be altruistic in his software development endeavors. After all, we can only eat ramen and live with our parents for so long!

However, for this project Weir's goal wasn't to make something that would be profitable. If that was his goal, he says, he would've approached it differently. The goal was to explore how to replicate the natural properties of paint using a web browser and, as he says, "make something awesome."

When detractors said that there was no sense in spending time on Viscosity because it wouldn't make him any money, it had no effect. Weir knew that wasn't the goal of the project in the first place. He understood the purpose of Viscosity and set out with a clear understanding of what he wanted to achieve. This allowed him to ignore negative comments and see his idea come to fruition. That's the power of vision!

Seeing Viscosity come to life was Weir's goal. He says that creation can be as important as the end product. He built Viscosity because the idea interested him and he enjoyed the challenge. In this case, he didn't need a business plan or elaborate strategy. To Weir, Viscosity was a creative exercise:

> Creativity is like a muscle. You have to flex it. And, a lot of times, it's not about doing it right. It's about doing it.

So consider spending some free time fleshing out various ideas. Take a break from your ongoing projects and allow yourself to be creative with as few constraints as possible.

Steal (I Mean Borrow) from Others

But what if you're tired and out of ideas? The blank canvas can be a scary proposition. If you're under the gun or feeling uninspired, then let's not reinvent the wheel. We should make it a practice to look at others' work for new ideas.

In *Steal Like an Artist: 10 Things Nobody Told You About Being Creative* (Workman), author Austin Kleon suggests we have to free ourselves from the pressures of being original:

> If we're free from the burden of trying to be completely original, we can stop trying to make something out of nothing, and we can embrace influence instead of running away from it.

So often we needlessly pressure ourselves to be original or innovative and we actually hamper our creativity. Today we have access to millions of websites, mobile applications, gaming systems, television menus, ebook readers, shopping kiosks, and many other user experiences. We should be relentlessly studying these interfaces and searching for new possibilities within our own applications. However, I see many developers throw out their early ideas with a quick dismal of, "that's already been done." They toil and wander the barren landscape of their ideas looking for the oasis of an original idea. Many times they never find one, and because of this, they never reach an innovative breakthrough.

In the literary world, great writers know that if you want to write well, you need to write. Write constantly, and when you're not writing, read. You should read works from the masters and examine how they weave together their stories. Learn from their style and prose and continually examine your own. Great writers aren't concerned about others' influence on their work; they remain confident that their own creativity will shine through.

In the book *The Writer's Idea Workshop* (Writers Digest Books), Jack Heffron discusses how new writers struggle with the anxiety of influence:

> [Writers] fear they won't find their own unique voice. They fear their ideas will lack originality. This concern, I think, is vastly overrated. Most apprentices can benefit much more from that type of influence then by trying to avoid it. Your own voice will emerge. Your own ideas will break away from the master's ideas. In the meantime, you'll be learning the craft and learning how good writing works.

There are many parallels between writing a book and writing an application. Both processes require a great deal of personal creativity and resolve. They both involve receiving criticism and learning how to take feedback constructively and make the work better. Many developers, just like writers, fear there are no more original ideas and begin to block themselves from creative thinking.

This is what I say to developers when I see them thinking this way: "There may be plenty of Twitter apps, but there are none of *your* Twitter apps." Each of us has the ability to bring our personal experience, programming knowledge, preferences, and user base to a particular application. The very nature that you are working on it makes it different.

I'm not saying that you shouldn't challenge yourself to innovate and improve applications that are already available; I'm saying that because something already exists, it shouldn't prevent you from exploring your idea.

If Michael Crichton had decided there were too many books about dinosaurs, he may never have written *Jurassic Park*. If Anne Rice had believed that vampires had become too passé, she may not have written *Interview with the Vampire*.

Not too long ago I was working with a colleague as we went through some new design concepts for our company portal. We were discussing several ideas about how search results could include employees' contact information. We were finding it difficult to imagine ways we could display search results that promoted this type of information. Then, my colleague suggested that we look at how Facebook handles its search results. We also looked at Google+ and Twitter (Figure 6-1 is a result of that discussion).

Looking at how these companies handled social search and relevancy spurred new ideas for our project. We weren't directly stealing what these companies had done. Instead we were learning from what they had already implemented. We took the ideas that made sense for our project and discarded the ones that didn't. After all, our project was dealing with employees' professional contacts. However, we were able to observe parallels with how Facebook, for instance, dealt with personal contacts in search results.

We should also be cataloging the things we find interesting. If you're using an application that has a unique way of logging in, take a screenshot and file it away for future use. You might not be working on a login screen right now, but maybe you will be in a few months.

In time, you should have a physical or virtual drawer that you can return to when creativity is low. Surround yourself with creative people and observe what they're doing. You might not have Vincent van Gogh living next door to you, but there are plenty of Twitter accounts, blogs, books, and videos on the Internet. Find where those sites are, bookmark them, and return to them periodically: see Chapter 11 for a good list to help you get started.

Keep your collection organized and thoughtful. Don't just throw together a bunch of haphazard screenshots, clippings, and articles. Kleon suggests that your creativity will only be as good as what you surround yourself with:

> My mom used to say to me, "Garbage in, garbage out." It used to drive me nuts. But now I know what she meant.
>
> Your job is to collect good ideas. The more good ideas you collect, the more you can choose from to be influenced by.

One tool that helps me collect great designs is the website Dribbble (*http://dribb ble.com/*). Essentially Dribbble is show-and-tell for designers. Artists and illustrators post whatever they're working on and users can comment, like, and follow them.

I created an account, and every so often, I'll peruse the site looking for things that I enjoy or find interesting. All I have to do is like something, and it gets moved to a list where I can recall it later. It's the perfect drawer for ideas. Additionally, Dribbble gives me the ability to search for whatever I might be interested in. Just the other day, a friend and I were searching Dribbble for ideas about how an audio player should look in his application.

Another site, Pinterest (*http://pinterest.com/*), has similar functionality, but it features a more broad collection of art. With Pinterest you and your friends can "pin" anything on the Web that strikes your fancy. Perhaps it's a funny t-shirt or an interesting use of typeface. Maybe it's an inspiring quote or unique piece of furniture. Pinterest is a great way to collect ideas, and because it's broader in scope than Dribbble, it exposes you to other influences. Believe it or not, I've actually used the style of a chair as inspiration for a website I was working on.

Creating delightful user experiences will require this kind of dedication, but it doesn't have to be a lonesome quest. By asking questions of your users, you can bring them along for the journey as well.

Creativity Requires Questioning

You might be starting to see a common theme throughout our discussion. User-centered design is a relentless pursuit for answers, and a good designer or developer never stops asking *why*. Browsing sites like Dribbble and Pinterest will have little impact if you're not taking the time to reflect on what you find. While observing the work of others, you should be asking yourself questions like:

- Why was this product or service a success or failure?
- What's this website doing that its competitors aren't? Is this the better approach?
- What is it about this application's design or layout that I like or don't like?
- Why does this product frustrate me? What would I do to make it better?

We need to be able to articulate the reasons why we like or don't like something. When a design isn't working, we should be able to express what's going wrong; and when we don't have the right language, we should read blogs, articles, and books by those who do. So many developers I've met can spend hours ranting about a product's design flaws, but when prompted for ideas on how they would improve it, they go strangely quiet.

Like any great user-centered developer, you can also ask questions of the people around you. We've all been there when someone is frustrated using a mobile phone, ATM, website, or any other product. A user's frustration is a gold mine of creative insight. Behind every "This sucks!" or "Who made this thing?" is a wealth of information we can use to avoid design flaws in our own projects. However, all is lost if we're unwilling to listen. Great developers and designers are constantly asking questions and observing human behavior.

When visiting my local mall or shopping center, I like to walk around and people watch. I like to see what types of smartphones people are using, or I may watch customers as they fiddle with a self-checkout register. Sometimes, if they don't look too busy, I might stop and ask them what they think of the product they're using: "What do you like most about it?"; "What do you wish it did better?"; "Would you recommend it to your friend?" Once I eavesdropped on a lady behind me at a restaurant as she was talking to a friend about why she took her television back (it was too difficult to set up). Don't be afraid to ask others why they like or don't like something. Ask your coworkers what they think about a new service they discovered or game they've been playing. Most people I've met have an opinion they don't mind sharing. Often people feel honored that you care what they think; I find it amazing what insights I get from those types of discussions.

Another trove of usability information is your hairdresser. I've asked all the women at my local salon various questions about their smartphones or favorite websites. After all, I'm just sitting there while they cut my hair—what else would we talk about? They now know me as "the computer guy." Every time I come in, they have new stories to share about technology they've discovered.

But it's not always that easy.

We have to remember that, as software developers, we tend to be pretty technical. Our perceptions are skewed. Technical things just make sense to us and are second nature. While technology may come easily to us, I don't think that's representative of the regular population.

For a lot of people, technology is just a means to an end. They could care less whether it's there or not. If it serves a purpose and has value, then great; otherwise, they could live without it. You may find that everyday people have very few opinions about the products and services they use. It's just not something they think about. Still, if you're asking the right questions, you can coach these people into giving you useful information.

For instance, a friend of mine recently purchased a new smartphone. Our discussion went something like this:

> "Oh, you got the [latest smartphone model]!"
>
> "The what?"
>
> "Your new phone—that's the one running [the latest smartphone operating system]. What do you think?"
>
> "Oh, yeah. Um, it's OK. I just wanted a phone that took pictures, so this is the one they said I should get."

Of course, my mind melted. I wanted to expand on all the possibilities she now had available to her. I wanted to show her how she could stream music and videos, download apps, or play the latest online multiplayer game.

But then I realized she just wanted to take pictures on her phone, so I changed my line of questioning.

> "Do you like taking pictures more on your phone than on your camera?"
>
> "Yeah. I do. It's better."
>
> "Really? Why?"
>
> "Because I can easily share them with my friends and family on Facebook. I love Facebook. It makes it really easy to share. Sometimes that's a bit scary too though."

That launched us into a lengthy discussion about the merits of social networks and the risks of sharing personal information. I learned what aspects of Facebook she valued most. I realized that we viewed the service differently and that the features that were important to me she rarely used. It was an important reminder that although I'm not necessarily concerned about online privacy, others find it to be a challenging proposition.

Did this conversation have a direct link to the projects I was currently working on? No. However, discussions like these make me a more informed programmer and they expose me to others' perspectives and values. By learning how others use technology, I eventually convert that knowledge into new insights and better user experiences within my applications. Of course, all of this requires that I step out of my shell.

In order to be creative, we have to be willing to take risks. We have to explore subjects that are not normally in our area of interest. We have to try new foods and read different books—and by different I don't mean books about a different programming language. We need to travel to new places and talk to different people; we need to ask new questions and watch different kinds of movies. Sure, our peers might think it's a bit strange that we drew some pictures for our latest project. They may give us weird looks when we come into the lunch room holding food from that foreign restaurant that just opened.

That's OK, because creativity takes guts. It requires us to be uncomfortable, and it requires us to make mistakes. I think American filmmaker Woody Allen says it best:

> If you're not failing every now and again, it's a sign you're not doing anything very innovative.

If you find yourself failing and even a little embarrassed, it's a good sign that you're on the right path to your most innovative ideas.

The Short Version

- Make sure to include user experience goals in your user-centered design process. Your users expect more than basic functionality: they expect applications that are delightful and thoughtfully considered.

- Creativity requires us to be courageous and vulnerable. Although trying new things may be risky and embarrassing, it's the key to discovering new insights.

- Drawing and sketching can have a positive impact on your creativity. Also, consider encouraging your users to draw. This may help them communicate their ideas.

- Freedom from constraints is essential to encouraging creativity. Take a break from whatever you're currently working on and consider spending time exploring new projects, technologies, or interests.

- Fully understanding your goal or vision will help you remain focused and creative.
- If you're having trouble coming up with your own ideas, don't be afraid to observe others' work and incorporate it.
- Creativity requires you to constantly ask questions.

CHAPTER 7

Design Principles

"People ignore design that ignores people."
—Frank Chimero

Studying others' work can inspire our creativity, but studying and understanding design principles will protect us from making mistakes. Design principles are the scientific laws of the usability world, much like the laws of gravity and relativity in the world of physics. Design principles are fairly constant and have been crafted over many years from the study of cognition and human behavior. They help us by providing guidance based on humans' understanding and interpretations of their surroundings.

Having a good grasp of design principles and predictive models can help you effectively critique your work. It's the perfect language to express what's right or wrong with a design. Additionally, you can use these principles to educate your users, who often have a hard time expressing what they need. Help them find the right terminology by explaining the meaning of various design principles. It will give you both a common and correct language to work from.

It's impossible to outline all of the usability principles in this book, since many of them go beyond the scope of our discussion. Consider this a high-level view of some of the most recognizable principles.

Principle of Proximity (Gestalt Principle)

The principle of proximity is one of many principles defined in the *Gestalt principles of perception*. While you should study all the Gestalt principles, I think the *proximity principle* has the greatest potential impact for your applications and requires the least amount of effort.

The principle states that we perceive relationships between objects that are closer together. Conversely, objects that are further apart would, seemingly, have less relation.

Because of this, you may hear the principle of proximity referred to as the grouping principle. Basically, it's easier to see patterns of operation when items are grouped together based on their function, as demonstrated in Figure 7-1.

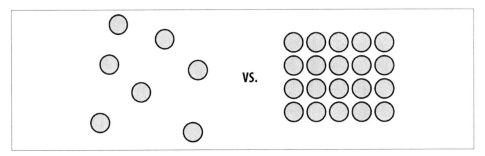

Figure 7-1. An example of the proximity principle, with the group on the right appearing related

This is why the proximity principle can have the greatest impact. By simply organizing and grouping items in a way that describes their function, you can significantly improve the user's experience with your application. An organized layout makes learning your application easier, and it puts less strain on the user to find things. Many developers miss this simple principle because they haven't taken the time to consider how their application should be organized. They think their application layout makes sense; meanwhile, their users are confused and frustrated. The proximity principle can be used as a powerful indicator that certain features belong together.

Consider the Microsoft Office suite of applications. In 2007, Microsoft introduced the Ribbon interface, which was a grouping of Office functions along the top of an application's window. This interface was a result of users becoming increasingly confused about the location of certain Office features. Microsoft introduced the Ribbon as a way to put similar functions in closer relation to one another.

For example, in the Word Ribbon, which is depicted in Figure 7-2, functions that alter the style of text are put in close proximity, as are functions that manipulate images, functions that change the layout of the document, and so on. Additionally, Microsoft made the Ribbon contextual, so the Ribbon actually changes based on the item that's selected in the document. This helps users by surfacing more relevant features based on the content they are manipulating.

Figure 7-2. Microsoft Word Ribbon interface

Nothing is more frustrating than a disorganized application. It requires the user to hunt and peck through complex menus and options, looking for the virtual needle in a haystack. This reduces our efficiency and our patience. Organizing an application by proximity helps users understand how your application functions and allows them to quickly assess the options that are available.

Visibility, Visual Feedback, and Visual Prominence

Visibility is really anything you use to bring visual focus to an element or action in your application's user interface. There are a variety of ways to do this:

Typeface
Different styles and sizes of text can draw a user's attention.

Opacity
Adjusting an item's opaqueness helps reduce or enhance its visibility.

Prominence
Those elements that are larger than others will bring them greater visibility, as demonstrated in Figure 7-3.

Status
Indicates that the application is processing a request or has received input from the user.

Color/Contrast
Traditionally, items with higher contrast or brighter colors will draw more attention.

Figure 7-3. Example of prominence, one of the visibility principles

The visibility principle can be used when you indicate the status of an application. For instance, the messaging client I use at work has an icon that turns gray to indicate when I'm no longer signed in, as shown in Figure 7-4. Upon signing in, it turns green. This small change helps me stay informed of my status while using the service.

Figure 7-4. My messaging client provides a green indicator to let me know I'm currently available for chat

Another aspect of the visibility principle is providing visual feedback. The visual feedback principle states that applications should respond to the user's input. In other words, your application should display some indication that it has received information from the user. A simple example of this would be providing a spinning wheel icon or a "searching..." message when a user submits a search query. The overall point of the visual feedback principle is to notify the user that an interaction has occurred. Without this confirmation, the user is left confused about whether or not their action was received by the application.

Most applications provide feedback to the user. However, I've seen some poor implementations of it. For instance, Figure 7-5 shows how my university's course catalog system responds when I search for a particular class.

On the first day of registration, I was convinced that the search engine was broken because I would submit a search query and nothing would happen. It took a few minutes before I noticed the spinning wheel in the upper-right corner. In this case the system was providing visual feedback, but because it was poorly positioned, I completely missed it.

Additionally, because of the increased traffic of everyone registering at the same time, the system was slow to respond. This meant that visual feedback was even more important because queries were taking longer than normal. A more appropriate placement of the spinning wheel would've been near the search button, which is where my eyes were focused when I submitted my query. With this more appropriate placement, I would've clicked the search button and immediately seen my query being processed.

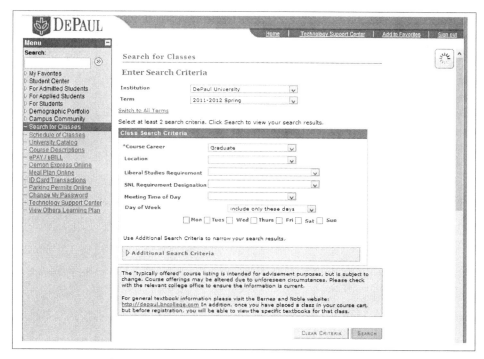

Figure 7-5. DePaul University's course catalog search interface

Issues with visibility and proper visual feedback are the most common usability issues I see in applications. Anytime I hear a user complaining that an interface is confusing or difficult to figure out, I start examining ways I might be violating visibility principles.

Your application should be continually providing appropriate status messages. Never make a user wonder if your application is still working. If your application requires some processing time to complete a request, make sure you're indicating that to the user.

Hierarchy

In developing more complex systems, it can become difficult to organize all of your application's features. The hierarchy principle, or visual hierarchy, states that applications should provide visual indicators to assist the user in perceiving how the application is organized. Most often than not, this takes the form of flyout menus and other navigational elements. It can also be applied by using the proximity principle discussed earlier in this chapter.

I've worked on projects that have had incredibly difficult hierarchies. The hardest part for the developer is trying to organize your application in a meaningful way. You can spend hours trying to determine where a particular feature belongs or what it should be called.

One tool that has been invaluable for these types of challenges is *affinity diagramming*, which is the process of laying out your application's features (typically with sticky notes) and organizing them into meaningful groups.

I like to use brightly colored sticky notes like those shown in Figure 7-6 because they make my grouping more visual. I also use markers to put dots on the notes to indicate other things I want to see. The colors of the markers and sticky notes make it easy to quickly see patterns, and the adhesive of the notes allow me to try different arrangements.

Figure 7-6. An example of an affinity diagram using colored sticky notes

In laying out our company portal, this type of diagramming was useful in seeing all of the features we wanted to make available to our users. There were hundreds of sections, policies, applications, and websites. With affinity diagramming, it made the challenge more digestible and it provided a way for us to quickly try different patterns of organization.

Mental Models and Metaphors

Whether we realize it or not, when confronted with a new application or product, we apply our knowledge from other products to conceptualize how it may work. In effect, our previous experiences shape our understanding of how the world works.

For example, the computer functions Cut and Paste rely on our familiarity with cutting paper into pieces and gluing them together. In fact, most applications indicate the Cut feature with a depiction of a pair of scissors. This icon helps re-enforce the metaphor of the Cut function because most of us know how scissors work. If we had never used the Cut feature in an application before, we could see the scissor icon and make a safe assumption about its purpose.

But what happens when our mental model misleads us?

In his book *The Design of Everyday Things* (Basic Books), Donald Norman explains the challenge of misleading mental models by describing household appliances:

> Home furnaces, air conditioners, and even most household ovens have only two levels of operation: full power or off. Therefore, they are always heating or cooling to the desired temperature as rapidly as possible. In these cases, setting the thermostat too high does nothing but waste energy when the temperature overshoots the target.

Here's an example: a woman checks into her hotel and finds her room unbearably hot. She walks over to the air conditioner control, and it reads a stifling 87°F! In her desperate attempt to get cool she presses the down arrow on the control until it reaches the minimum setting of 50°F. Her mental model of the air conditioner is incorrect. She believes that by setting the control to its coldest setting, she will get the room to her desired temperature more quickly. In reality, the air conditioner can only apply cooling at fixed rates—usually high and low. By setting the conditioner to its coldest setting, she only ensured that it would get much colder than she desired.

As developers we need to be aware of the mental models users are applying to our applications. Icons and language should accurately represent how our applications function. I've seen many developers choose inappropriate icons for applications. Without realizing it, they've implied a certain purpose, and when users click on the icon, they are confused by the outcome.

For instance, if you're building a travel-booking website, you might think having a coconut for a search button would be cute and fun. Unfortunately, users don't have a conceptual model of how a coconut applies. A magnifying glass has a closer relationship to searching for something. This is because many of us know that in the real world magnifying glasses are used to scan text in books and periodicals. Although I encourage you to challenge conventional wisdom and push innovation, some models should be left intact.

Another interesting mental model is the notion of Save within applications. Some of us are familiar with the traditional floppy disk as being the icon for saving files on a computer. This model was generated from older computers that used 3.5-inch floppy drives for saving documents.

Younger generations are unfamiliar with this model because many of them have never used a floppy disk. Once, I heard a boy refer to the Save icon as a "boxy thingy." It was not only amusing, but also a powerful reminder of the importance of mental models. I imagine that at some point we'll have to come up with an updated representation for the activity of saving documents on a computer. As we move to the concepts of the cloud for everyday storage, even mental models like documents and folders will become dated as well.

How do you think we could improve these metaphors? Interesting indeed!

Progressive Disclosure

Progressive disclosure is a great way to help users understand what features are available to them within your application. By simply hiding options that are not possible, you can reduce users' cognitive load and guide them more effectively through their tasks. The progressive disclosure principle is a rather easy thing to employ and is especially useful in more complex applications with feature-laden menus.

For example, Adobe Photoshop, a professional photo-editing software, is full of features and tools for designers. If Adobe did not incorporate progressive disclosure, all of those features would appear to be available, regardless of what I was doing within the application. This would put a significant burden on me as I tried to discover what is and is not possible. Instead, Adobe grays out and disables items that are not applicable to my current situation, as you see in Figure 7-7. This subtle indicator provides a powerful aid in helping me navigate the many possibilities of Photoshop.

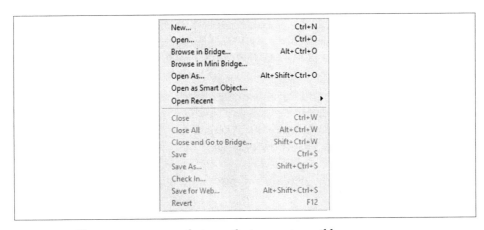

Figure 7-7. This menu grays out features that are not possible

Consistency

The principle of consistency may seem obvious, but I've seen it overlooked by many developers. This principle maintains that users learn and understand applications more easily when they are consistent with what they already know. I've seen developers introduce new methods for completing tasks that have already been well established.

For instance, I remember an application that required me to create a preview of my document before printing it. In every application I've used up to that point, I'd never been required to create a preview of a document before printing it. The developers may have had good intentions for this workflow. Perhaps they thought it'd be best to ensure I viewed a preview of my document so I'd be less likely to print something I didn't want. However, this design was inconsistent with what I already knew. I can appreciate the developers trying to improve on the printing process, but in this case, the act of creating a preview before printing was not obvious to me and created unnecessary confusion.

Again, I would always encourage looking for new ways to accomplish tasks within an application. However, you should be leery of introducing new workflows that are inconsistent with common understandings. And if you do introduce something new, make sure it's better than what we already know!

An example of this is how FiftyThree implemented the action of Undo in Paper for the iPad.

The user can take two fingers, place them on the screen, and begin moving in a counterclockwise (Undo) or clockwise (Redo) motion. Other applications provide a button for Undo. However, FiftyThree decided a button did not fit its vision for Paper. The company believed that looking for and pressing a button was unnecessary and took users out of their creative flow.

So, FiftyThree decided it was going to improve the Undo process. To do that, it had to look at new ways for implementing it. It studied other industries to gain new insights into how undoing work could be done. That's when it uncovered how filmmakers undo their work, as Petschnigg explains.

> Our interaction designer, Andrew Allen—who's a filmmaker—he's been working a lot with jog dials on VCRs. And for him, it was like, "We need rewind. We don't need Undo, we need Rewind!"
>
> And that's, kind of, where that gesture came from. And it really fit into our way of thinking about—sort of—what does mobile creation look like? How should an app work when you're on the go? How do we keep people in their work and, rather than having to bring up a menu, find a little button—it's like it flows really naturally.

The developers at FiftyThree could've just looked at what their competitors were doing and assumed that a traditional Undo button was the standard that all users had come to understand. They could've been conservative and saved time by not evaluating their pre-conceived notions about how Undo should work.

Instead, the team focused on their goal to create an application that encouraged creativity. The way they saw it, the Undo paradigm was an attack on their mission. So they had intense discussions about what some would deem a trivial function. They explored how the current way of undoing work was disjointed by requiring the discovery and use of menus and buttons. They explored other industries and how they handled manipulating creative work. Through all of that, they came up with an incredible insight: we didn't need Undo; we needed Rewind.

So, as with many things, there's no easy answer. Consistency within your applications is critical because it reduces your users' cognitive burden and eases them into learning how your application works. Nothing is worse than having to relearn basic functions because the developer thought it'd be neat to do things differently.

Sometimes it's nice when an application behaves how you expect it to, when a menu item is exactly where you'd expect it to be, or an action has the proper outcome. Other times, as in the case of undoing work with Paper, it's delightful to be surprised and experience something different.

Balancing consistency in your design can be challenging, but if it's done correctly, it can create an application that is easy to learn and enjoyable to use.

Affordance and Constraints

Many objects, such as tools and household appliances, are designed to afford us their proper use and constrain us from using them improperly. These are the principles of affordance and constraints. An example of this is the three-pronged electrical plug and outlet. These objects are designed to not only complement each other, but also work one way. It's virtually impossible to plug in a three-pronged electrical plug, shown in Figure 7-8, the wrong way. With its flat prongs and round post, the plug makes it immediately clear to people how to use it. And if it's not clear, it prevents them from plugging it in wrong and hurting themselves!

At the hospital we have a saying: "Make it easy to do the *right thing* and difficult to the *wrong thing*." Affordance makes it easy to do the right thing, while constraints make it difficult to do the wrong thing.

Figure 7-8. Three-prong electrical plug

If you're observing users making mistakes in your application, consider limiting options or anticipating their workflow. Develop actions that function in a way that make it impossible to do the wrong thing. Users will appreciate you looking out for them and will have greater trust in your application.

Confirmation

One way to prevent users from doing the wrong thing is by asking for confirmation. The confirmation principle states that an application should prevent undesired actions by requesting verification, as demonstrated in Figure 7-9.

Figure 7-9. This little guy has saved me more than once

In most applications, if I'm working with a document and try to close it without saving, a prompt will be displayed. Usually it asks if I'd like to save before exiting the program.

If I select Cancel and try to close the application again, the prompt will return. Essentially there's no way for me to close the application without first addressing whether or not I want to save the document. This protects me from doing the wrong thing and losing my work.

Be sure that your application anticipates an undesired action. Nothing will make your users hate you more than allowing them to unintentionally lose their work.

Hick's Law

Hick's Law is a prescriptive model that helps you calculate the time it takes for users to make a decision as a result of the number of choices they have. It's also known as reaction time, or RT, and is represented mathematically like this:

$$RT = a + b \log_2 N$$

The model can prove helpful when evaluating your menus to ensure they're not overloaded. A common question in application design is: "How many items should be present in a menu, and how should they be organized?"

For example, a company portal's navigational scheme can be extremely difficult to manage. Consider the company portal we discussed earlier in the principle of hierarchy. More than likely, users want whatever they're looking for to be the first item in the menu. After all, it's the most important because they're looking for it! See Figure 7-10 for an example.

Obviously, there can only be one first item, so being able to identify and prioritize items within a menu can be a tug-of-war battle.

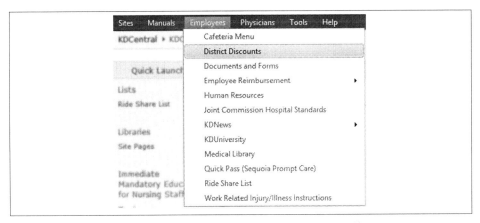

Figure 7-10. An example drop-down menu from our company portal

Therefore, because of its linear nature, Hick's Law suggests that we process information at a constant rate. In short, the more items you put in front of users, the more time it's going to take them to find what they're looking for.

It seems obvious, but I still see developers create applications or websites with incredibly complex navigational menus. I think it's easy for our applications to get away from us. We keep adding and adding, and before we know it, they become unmanageable. So we move and reorganize items to avoid having to do the difficult work of deciding what we should get rid of.

By applying the principle of hierarchy and using Hick's Law as a prescriptive model, we can better decide the value of each item within our menus.

Fitt's Law

Fitt's Law can help you determine the size of target elements, such as buttons, menus, etc., within your interface based on the distance a user's pointing device must travel. This prescriptive model is expressed in movement time, or MT, and proves that the farther the user must travel between two elements, the less precise the user will be reaching the target. If your intention is to have a user click on a button, the size of that button will be dictated by the distance between the button and the user's cursor. The equation is given here:

$$MT = a + b\log_2(2A/W)$$

Imagine if Google made its search buttons Google Search and I'm Feeling Lucky smaller and off to the side, as shown in Figure 7-11. That would increase the distance between the search box, where our cursor is, and the buttons, or target. Therefore, our accuracy would diminish, and our movement time would go up.

Figure 7-11. Users wouldn't be happy with this design change!

The distance users have to travel from an object should dictate the size of the object they are moving to. Fitt's Law is correlative. In other words, the farther the distance a user must travel, the larger the target objects should be. The exact size is determined by the acceptable movement time.

Fitt's Law is useful for mouse-driven interfaces; however, there have been new studies that have adjusted the model to accommodate touch-driven interfaces as well.

The Short Version

- It's important to learn and study design principles. There are many, and by simply following their guidance, you can dramatically improve the experience of your applications.
- The principle of proximity states that humans perceive a relationship between objects that are closer together. Use this principle by grouping functions together. This will make it easier to learn and understand your application.
- The visibility principle states that visual cues should be present to assist users in understanding the status of the application.
- The visual prominence principle states that a user's attention is drawn to objects that are larger, brighter, or more prominent.
- The principle of visual feedback states that an application should respond to the user by signifying that an input has been received. Applications should also indicate to the user when they are processing a request.
- Mental models and metaphors are how humans transfer real-world knowledge to the computing world. Be sure that your iconography, language, and other metaphors are rooted in knowledge users understand.
- Progressive disclosure removes and disables features that are not applicable to the user's current state.
- The consistency principle states that tasks within an application should function as expected. You shouldn't invent new workflows for completing tasks that are already understood by the user.
- Affordance helps users do the right thing, and constraints prevent them from doing the wrong thing.
- The confirmation principle states that applications should require verification to prevent users from performing undesired actions. The save confirmation dialog is a good example.
- Hick's Law is a prescriptive model that's used to determine the time it takes to select an item based on the number of items available to choose from. The more items you include in a menu, the longer the response time is for the user.
- Fitt's Law is another prescriptive model that's used to determine the time it takes a user to move the cursor from one location to the target location. The further a user must travel with their cursor, the less accuracy the user will have in reaching the target object.

CHAPTER 8

Gathering Feedback

"Millions saw the apple fall, but Newton was the
one who asked why."

—Bernard Mannes Baruch

It's time to go out into the world and find out what users really think about the applications we make for them. We need to ask detailed questions and open ourselves to criticism that may be difficult to hear. We have to observe users and document our findings in order to gain an overall understanding of what works and what doesn't.

Receiving criticism is not fun. If anyone has told you they enjoy getting feedback on their work, that person is lying. Being told you missed something, made a mistake, or went in the wrong direction essentially means you're not finished. It means you have more work to do. It means you're not perfect.

I'm not going to tell you to enjoy criticism. I'm not going to say you should shout with glee at the thought of redesigning an application or that you should do a happy dance when you realize you'll have to recode a complex function.

The truth is that we all want to hit a home run. We want to show our new application to users, clients, friends, and family and be told we've nailed it: we got everything right, we're done, and we did it all on version 1.0.

Here's what I will suggest: we have to learn to be tolerant of feedback. The best developers I know have a desire to get things right, no matter the consequence. Above all else (sleep, money, or ego), they want to build the best application possible. They realize that receiving honest, quality feedback is the only way to get there, and here's the kicker—they actually ask for this feedback. I didn't say they enjoyed it, but they do value it. These developers get their applications into the hands of potential users as soon as possible. They ask them detailed questions and encourage them to be brutally honest. They survey the marketplace, look at their competitors, and revise their applications to ensure they provide competitive value.

I spend all my time and earn my livelihood from writing code; I absolutely love doing it. In my opinion, it's the best part of building any application. The act of creating a functioning product from nothing is, to put it mildly, addicting. If you don't have the desire to write code, it's impossible for you to be a successful developer. How else could you muster the energy to spend a week trying to get an event trigger just right?

When I'm working inside code, I'm comfortable, and as odd as it sounds, it provides me the least resistance. I can plunk away at keys and become hyper-focused on getting features to work. The problem with this approach is I never stop to consider, "Do users even *want* this feature?" I know I should spend time with my users first, and I know I should be asking questions and creating a plan of action. Instead, I end up saying things like, "I just want to see if [programming challenge] is possible first." I tell myself, time and again, that I'll go back to a more structured software development process as soon as I get [programming challenge] working. When I do this, I set myself up for failure.

I often remind myself that I'll get to the code in due time, but before that, I need to get some questions answered. I need to gain a fundamental understanding of what I'm trying to build. Sure, I might have a general idea, but I need to make sure I've worked out the specifics. It's impossible to effectively discover what my application is going to be while I'm writing it. If I want to be successful and create an application users are going to want to use, I have to be disciplined and patient.

If you're currently working on an application, I challenge you to answer the following fundamental questions:

- What problem does your application solve? What's its core focus?
- Who are the ideal users for your application? What are they like? Are they advanced users or novices?
- What are your three must-have features? How do you know they are the most important?
- How will your application provide value? How will it improve on what people are currently using?

If you can't easily answer some of these questions, don't fret. Most developers I know have a hard time with them. The truth is that if we're only focused on getting features to work, it's impossible to maintain perspective on the overall vision and purpose of our application. This is why I suggest developers embrace user-centered design, which is why I wrote this book! Only by allowing users to continually give us feedback can we test our assumptions and ensure we're moving in the right direction.

However, it's much more than just asking users to share their opinions. We have to be methodical, almost anthropological, in our study. We need to ask our users for input and observe their behaviors. This way, we can learn from what they're telling us and catch the things they're not.

Let's take a look at some tools we can use to collect feedback and observe our users effectively.

How Many Users Will I Need?

First, you might be asking yourself how many study subjects you should have to produce meaningful feedback. As with any great question, the answer is that it depends. It really depends on what you're trying to achieve and what value you plan to put on the results.

In some cases, I'll start out with some pretty informal questioning. I might ask only a handful of people some questions about their needs in a particular problem space. I realize that their feedback might not be representative of the larger user base, so I take that into context when reviewing their responses.

I would argue that the mix far outweighs the quantity. In other words, get information from a diverse set of people. Developers often seek feedback amongst their peers. There's nothing wrong with that, but we have to realize that our developer friends tend to evaluate our work from a technical perspective. Obviously, if the target audience for your application is developers, then it makes sense to capture feedback from developers at all ranges of experience.

If I'm building an application for nursing managers to organize staffing for each shift, I'll want to gather feedback from a mixture of people involved with the nurse staffing process. I might survey nurse managers, registered nurses, licensed nurses, nursing directors, and unit coordinators. This could be a group as few as 5 or as many as 30. It just depends on how many resources I have available to me. It wouldn't make sense to test the application with my developer colleagues. They may provide some useful feedback, but it would be lacking the real-world knowledge of a nursing professional.

How you recruit your subjects can also affect the legitimacy of your sample. Let's say you're building a website for seniors to help them learn about their health benefits. You want to know how comfortable seniors are with using the Web, so you send out a survey via email. By sending an email survey you may be targeting the wrong group. Sure, they might be in the desired age range, but the fact that they're using email might put them in a particular group, namely people who are comfortable using computers. To ensure we're getting feedback from a diverse group of seniors, we might consider sending an email and printed survey. This way, our design decisions will be based on seniors who are comfortable and not so comfortable using computers.

Many studies have been done to discover the magic number of people that makes a sample statistically viable. While there is some industry debate on this issue, renowned usability expert Jakob Nielsen believes that you can achieve the best results with a minimum of five users. He states that a majority of usability errors will be discovered by the first five users and little is learned after that, as shown in Figure 8-1. Therefore, studying more than five users doesn't add additional value. If anything, it makes the study more complex and unmanageable

Think of when you order a pizza. The first slice is always the best because it provides you the most enjoyment. If you were hungry, you might be willing to pay $5 for it. The sixth (if you can eat as much pizza as I can) is simply not as enjoyable, and the chances are that you would be less willing to pay $5 for it. Therefore, the sixth slice of pizza is just not as valuable as the first.

Nielsen suggests that adding users to your study has the same effect. Adding more users just increases the complexity of the study and doesn't really offer as much value as the first five.

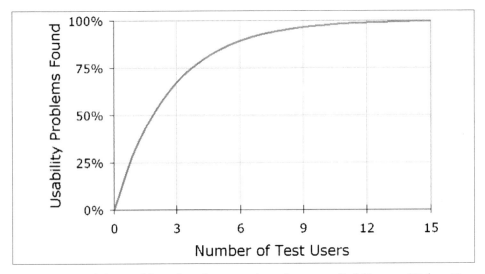

Figure 8-1. Usability problems found per number of users studied (Source: Nielsen Norman Group)

So, with all of that said, I think if you can gather between 5 to 10 subjects to observe while using your application, you'll discover some meaningful insight into what could be improved.

Notice the graph in Figure 8-1. If you don't study a single subject, you can expect to discover *zero usability problems*. That number seems to be the most guaranteed.

Surveys

One way to get direct user feedback is by creating and collecting surveys. Surveys can be a powerful tool in reaching a broad spectrum of people in a short amount of time. There are plenty of websites and online tools to help you prepare and distribute surveys

(SurveyMonkey (*http://www.surveymonkey.com*) is one that I've used on many occasions).

Creating a valid and reliable survey is an art form. It really is! Not only do you have to know what questions to ask, but you also have to ask them in a way that gives you useful feedback. Having clear, concise, and impartial questions, as well as selecting the right group of people, is the key to a successful survey.

My personal preference for the style of survey questions is to use the Likert scale. Named after the scale's creator, Dr. Rensis Likert, it features a range of responses for each question. Here's an example:

> This book has helped me improve my application-development skills.
>
> a. Strongly Agree
>
> b. Agree
>
> c. Neither Agree nor Disagree
>
> d. Disagree
>
> e. Strongly Disagree

By providing a range of responses, Likert scales help you gain greater insight into how much a respondent agrees with a particular statement. This can be valuable when dealing with fence sitters, users who tell you everything is good when prompted for their opinion.

These types of ranges help respondents by structuring their answers and guiding them in qualifying their opinion. With Likert scales, you can cover a variety of response types:

Frequency
Always, Frequently, Sometimes, and Never

Importance
Very Important, Important, Somewhat Important, and Not at All Important

Value:
Very High, High, Medium, Low, and Very Low

Satisfaction
Completely Satisfied, Satisfied, Neutral, Dissatisfied, and Completely Dissatisfied

Ranking
5, 4, 3, 2, and 1

However, one downside to Likert scales is the potential for *acquiescence bias*, which is the tendency for respondents to agree with statements because it feels less confrontational or takes less effort. Often times you'll conduct a survey only to find that you have a bunch of users who are in complete agreement with what you're stating. That's not very useful information if you're trying to decide which feature you should spend your time on.

If you're concerned about agreement bias, you can always employ *top box scoring* in your calculations. With top box, you only consider those values that are the best or most desired.

For example, if you were asking users about the importance of having spellcheck in your application, you would only count those that marked Very Important and divide that number by the total number of respondents. This may seem extreme, but it will help you understand just how desired a particular feature is.

If you choose to use Likert scales, try your best to ask questions using clear and neutral language. The more difficult the question is to process—or the more extreme the statement—the more likely respondents will answer in a way that does not reflect their intentions.

For example, a question like this is too positively leaning:

> The messaging feature in IT Works is useful.
>
> a. Strongly Agree
>
> b. Agree
>
> c. Neither Agree nor Disagree
>
> d. Disagree
>
> e. Strongly Disagree

At first glance, it seems like we're trying to understand the usefulness of the messaging feature in IT Works. This question is understandable, but the formatting could lead to responses that are less viable. For example, what if users believe the messaging feature is valuable because in training they were told it was? We might mistake users' perception of value as an indication of how much they use the messaging feature.

A way we might fix this is by asking the question using the frequency scale:

> I use the messaging feature in IT Works:
>
> a. Throughout the day
>
> b. A few times a week
>
> c. A few times a month
>
> d. Almost never
>
> e. Never

By phrasing the question this way, we're getting to the heart of what we want to know. If we want to know how useful the messaging feature is, we should be asking how often it's used.

In order to improve readability in my surveys, I like to pick one or two Likert scales and stick with them. For instance, if I choose to use a frequency scale twice, I'm going to make sure the range of responses is the same. I also prefer to limit the range of responses to no more than five, and I make sure they are easy to decode. I don't want users intending to agree with a statement and accidentally disagreeing. By making statements brief and providing consistency in my choices of response, I allow respondents to quickly assess and complete my surveys.

Also, by mixing up your statements to reflect both positive and negative language, you'll cause respondents to pause and consider their responses. Do your best to strike an equal balance. A consistent survey is easy to read and understand, but with a dash of inconsistency it will keep respondents on their toes and engaged in the questioning.

You can collect open-ended answers, such as essay questions, but I find that many subjects don't want to take the time to complete them. Additionally, spelling errors, fragmented sentences, and unclear statements end up providing very little value. Like everything else, the use of essay questions will likely depend on the audience you're surveying.

Conducting Interviews

While surveys can reach a large audience with little effort, they only give you a broad understanding of your users' needs. No matter how careful you are with your survey process, it can still feel like you're making assumptions based on the results. While interviews are time intensive and reach a smaller audience, they offer more detailed information. Conducting interviews ensures that you capture the intent of the user's remarks. You can clarify misunderstood questions and pick up on nonverbal cues like body language and tone.

For the most part, there are three types of interviews: structured, unstructured, and contextual. They're also known respectively as formal interviews, informal interviews, and contextual inquiries. All three approaches have their pros and cons, but they all share the value of direct interaction. The differences between structured and unstructured interviews are minimal; however, contextual interviews are a bit different. It doesn't necessarily have to be an either/or. You can choose to use each method at different stages in your application's development.

When you begin researching your application, you might choose to conduct unstructured interviews to explore the problem space. Unstructured interviews allow for a more open dialog that's fitting for this type of exploration. The key to unstructured interviews is the level of informality. Not structuring your interview allows free-form ideas to emerge because you're having an open discussion about the problem space.

That's not to say that your discussion should be random. It's just less focused on formalities and consistency. Unstructured interviews are useful when you really don't know what questions to ask. Perhaps you have an idea for an application but haven't decided on any specific features yet. The goal of unstructured interviews is to talk to as many people as you can about the problem you're trying to solve.

Unstructured interviews allow for normal conversation. By asking users about the problem space and letting them speak freely, you'll be surprised by the insight you gain. It's quite possible that they'll mention an issue you were unaware of or a workaround they use that ends up being a differentiating feature in your application.

Opposite of the unstructured interview is the structured interview. While unstructured interviews encourage freedom and exploration, structured interviews value consistency. Typically, structured interviews are conducted using a script. Each user is asked the same questions in the same tone and in the same order, and their responses are carefully documented.

This level of formality is best when you need answers to specific questions. For instance, let's say you want to know how users feel about a new navigational menu in your application. In a structured interview, you can ask specific questions about the menu and make design decisions based on direct user feedback. Typically, structured interviews have a tendency to be quicker because you already know what questions you'd like to have answered.

If you plan to conduct structured interviews, I encourage you to commit to it. Prepare a script ahead of time and do your best to read from it consistently with each user. Focus only on the script and do your best to avoid distractions or side conversations. This will allow you to compare each user's response equally.

Much like structured and unstructured interviews, contextual inquiries require that you ask a series of questions. However, the process is much more intimate because you immerse yourself in the user's environment. Rather than holding interviews in a conference room or over the phone, the focus of a contextual inquiry is to ensure that you engage users in the environment where they'll be using your application. This type of study allows you to come in contact with the environmental factors that might affect your users' ability to use your application. These factors, such as lighting, noise, and ergonomics, can be wide reaching yet powerful in their effect on users' overall experience. Some users take these factors for granted and would never think to bring them up in an interview over the phone or in your office. Sometimes, it pays to go where your application is or will be used and see for yourself.

For an example, let's go back to my visitor directory application discussed in Chapter 3.

The visitor directory was a touch-based system, and to give proper feedback, I spent weeks crafting the perfect audible tone that would indicate an item had been pressed. I tried several tones and labored over finding the perfect pitch. One was too high and another too low. I even played around with creating my own tone using a synthesizer. It took forever to find a sound that I was happy with.

When I finally found an appropriate tone and finished the project, I installed the kiosk in the hospital's front lobby. It was then that I realized I had made a fundamental mistake.

Roughly 15 feet from the kiosk's location was a water fountain. With the sound of running water so close, you couldn't hear my application's auditory feedback!

I also realized that because you couldn't hear the tones, my visual feedback wasn't significant. You could barely see the button change color when it was pressed. Therefore, I had to make the color brighter to ensure that users could acknowledge the input, regardless if they heard the tone or not. The water fountain, although wonderful to look at, had dramatically affected the ability for visitors to use my application.

I also ramped up the volume of the tone so it could be heard over the fountain. That was a mistake. I discovered later that the volunteers who worked at the front lobby would often unplug the speakers. When I asked them why they were doing this, they said that the sound was too noisy and obnoxious when they were speaking to visitors.

The point of this story is if I had taken the time to explore the hospital's front lobby by conducting a contextual inquiry, I would've been tipped off to these environmental factors. I would've realized that the noise from the water fountain would impact the user's ability to receive appropriate feedback from my design. I would've also realized there was a limit to how loud my application could be before I started to annoy the staff.

Additionally, if I had conducted a focus group with visitors in a conference room, I would not expect any of them to bring up an issue with the water fountain. Instead, we would've spent time discussing features they would've liked to have in a directory. By not spending time in the environment where the visitor directory was going to be used, I missed key insights.

As they say, hindsight is 20/20. When I placed the kiosk in the front lobby, it was clear to everyone that there wasn't enough visual or audible feedback. However, when I tested the application in my quiet office, there was no way for me to know that visual and auditory feedback would be an issue. I could have chosen to beat myself up about it, but it's impossible to foresee all the variables that affect a user's experience with an application.

That's why it's important to engage in activities like contextual inquiries and user interviews. With each aspect of the user-centered design model, I broaden my window of understanding.

This requires that we get up from our desks, ask questions, walk around the environment, and explore the problem space for ourselves.

Task Analysis

There are two more types of analysis you can use to assess the effectiveness of your application, task analysis and heuristic evaluation

Task analysis is the study of each step for a given task. The point of this type of analysis is to fully understand all the steps required to complete a task to improve the process with our application. In Chapter 4, we talked about the usefulness of workflow diagrams. Task analysis is a great way to generate these types of models.

Unlike a contextual inquiry, it's not necessary to observe users as they engage in their task, although I would definitely recommend it. With task analysis, it's possible to gain understanding about a task simply by asking questions or reading a procedural manual.

The challenge of walking through a task analysis with users is that they often want to describe all the aspects of the task all at once. If you're not careful, your analysis will be marred with confusing steps that are out of sequence. Users do not always have the ability to explain the tasks they perform. All too often, they'll provide insignificant details or leave out critical steps. It's not their fault. They don't know that developers think in terms of loops and conditional statements. They don't understand that we're thinking about the task and trying to apply 1s and 0s to it.

Because of this, I like to use scenario-based questioning to get the story of the task. At the hospital my questioning will often sound like this:

> Okay, let's rewind. Say I got my arm lopped off and I just walked into the ER. What happens next?

It's a gruesome image—and provides a little comic relief—but it also helps users walk through a task and take it one step at a time. I also make sure to stop them if they get ahead of themselves and ask them to explain acronyms or industry terms.

Additionally, it's critical that you repeat your understanding to users. Often, it will sound something like this:

> So let me make sure I've got what you're saying. You said that your first step is to go over to the scanner, then you bring up the scanning application on the computer, then you...

It's amazing how easily we misinterpret what users explain to us. Only by repeating my perceptions can I make sure I've received their explanations correctly.

Heuristic Evaluation

Rather than focusing on a particular task, heuristic evaluation is the process of examining applications against a set of rules or guidelines. Pioneered by Jakob Nielsen, heuristic evaluations can occur with or without the user present. It's almost like the process of editing a written work, but instead of evaluating grammar and spelling guidelines, you're evaluating your application's effectiveness based on industry standards or principles.

There are a lot of resources available to give you guidance. For instance, Microsoft, Google, and Apple all have fairly strict guidelines for the design of applications on their platforms. These guidelines can help you understand what your application should and should not do. I've seen design guidelines that are very specific, right down to the pixel. They give you guidance on the position of user interface (UI) elements, use of animations, load times, terminology, and various other instructions.

For example, if users know that the Share button in iOS applications is used for sharing content via email, social networks, and other services, it would be unwise to create your own sharing mechanism that users would have to learn. In some cases, companies will actually reject the submission of your application if these guidelines aren't met. Software companies enforce these standards because they want to ensure their users have a consistent experience among applications. Therefore, it can be costly to not understand the guidelines of the development platform you are using.

The more familiar you become with the rules of the framework's design, the easier it will be for you to spot inconsistencies.

Storyboarding

Another way to get feedback early in the design process is by storyboarding, the practice of sketching an experience point by point. Storyboarding is often used in Hollywood to plan the steps of a movie scene.

Like sketching, storyboarding can seem intimidating, but I can't make this point enough: you don't need to be an artist to engage in storyboarding. If you can draw basic shapes or lines, then that's all you'll need. See Figure 8-2 for an example. The point of storyboarding is not to create amazingly artistic experiences. It's to begin formulating the progression of your application in a visual way. If you only know how to draw stick figures, then draw the entire process with stick figures!

Spend time thinking: "First, users will do this, then they're going to do this, then..." Unlike a dataflow or workflow diagram, storyboarding is far more visual. Your storyboards should include early sketches of UI elements. Also think about the layout and design of your application and how it will respond to users as they navigate your application: What does that look like? What screens might they see? Are there animations to cue them into the progression from one screen to another?

I've heard some folks refer to this process as pseudocoding, and in a way that makes sense. It's a way for us to start to code without actually writing in a coding language. Instead, we're using a visual language. It prepares us for all the possibilities and functionality that we will be required to code. With storyboarding, we get a 50,000-foot view of the application and we're left with a much clearer roadmap for where we're headed.

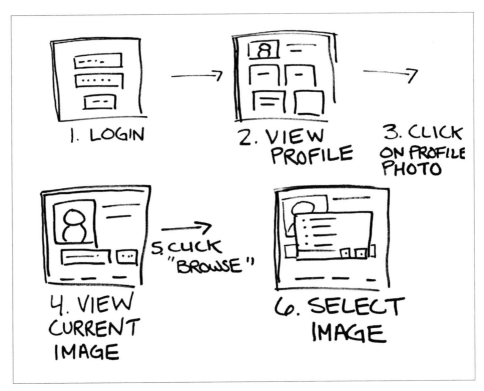

Figure 8-2. Storyboard on changing a user's profile photo

Storyboarding leads you to make early decisions about your application's layout and process. You'll begin to realize what concepts will and will not be necessary for a good user experience. Show your storyboards to your users and make sure the workflow meets their needs. This is a great way to root out any miscommunication and avoid costly design mistakes.

It may be tempting to use a software design tool for your storyboards. I'd argue against that. With storyboarding, the pen and paper are your best friends. With applications like Adobe Photoshop and QuarkXPress, you run the risk of focusing on the quality of the storyboard and not the quality of the user experience.

Storyboards can help you turn your development into a story, just like we learned from FiftyThree's narrative-based design process for Paper. Storyboarding helps you explore each step of your application and evaluate your design.

Try taking one of your application's workflows and creating a storyboard around it. How many steps are required? What screens are displayed? How does the user react to them? Is there any way to eliminate or combine screens to make the process easier?

Using Prototypes

Prototyping is the process of building low- or high-quality mockups of your application's design to have something tangible to test with users. Prototyping is a powerful way to help your users visualize what you intend to deliver through your application.

There is an incredible benefit that comes from seeing your early ideas take shape. Although prototypes can take time up front, they can save you hours of building something that ultimately doesn't work. They are a way to assess the visual design of your application without making a significant programming investment.

When you make the mistake of approaching your design from code, you're more apt to find solutions that are best for your code and not for the user experience. Prototyping frees you from thinking about the coding challenges and focuses you on the user's interaction with your application.

However, there is a danger in prototyping for us code-hungry developers. Prototyping can closely mimic the actual building of the application and can easily get out of hand.

Developer and designer Billy Hollis has a great way to know if your prototype has reached that point:

> If you've got unit testing in your prototype, you're doing it wrong.

That's not to suggest that pursuing a high-fidelity prototype is without merit. In some cases, software developers craft a semi-functional prototype that will eventually turn into the finished product.

The problem is that developers make the mistake of focusing on the prototype. They use it as a way to suggest they are testing the design; but in reality, they're just writing code. Additionally, developers may choose to build their prototype in their native development tool. I feel strongly that if you're building a prototype using your development tools (e.g., Microsoft Visual Studio, XCode, or some other popular integrated development environment) the temptation to submerge yourself in code becomes even greater.

There are other solutions (see Chapter 11) that are better designed for building functional prototypes. These software products give you the proper tools to ensure you're focusing on the right elements of your prototype. They make it easy to quickly adjust your layout, and they limit your ability to delve into elaborate programming. This keeps your focus away from code and instead on the application's visual and interactive design.

When considering the quality of your prototype, think about the perception the user will have about what development stage the application is in. The higher the fidelity or richness of the prototype can have implications on the type of feedback you'll receive from users.

For instance, if you place a polished prototype in front of a user and ask her to evaluate it, don't be surprised if she offers you little substantial insight. It's because the more functionality and design your prototype provides, the more likely she'll believe that it's near completion. No sense in providing feedback at this point—it looks like you're almost done!

She may not question some of the fundamental assertions you've made. She may have the misunderstanding that they've already been decided. Therefore, she'll only give you feedback on minor details.

However, if you place a low-fidelity prototype like the one shown in Figure 8-3 in front of her, the impression is that very little commitment has been made to the overall design. She'll feel more emboldened to question functionality and core concepts.

Figure 8-3. Usability testing using a paper prototype (Source: Luma Institute's public workshops)

Likewise, you are more willing to accept feedback when you've invested less time building your prototype. If a user tells you that you've missed a critical screen in your prototype, and you've only drawn it on paper, that's no problem! You'll just grab a new piece of paper, and in minutes, you've reorganized your prototype to explore that need. You'll spend less time defending your work and more time constructively working with the user—and that's exactly what you want to be doing.

When users don't know what they need, it's common to find yourself with what I call The Commissioned Artist Syndrome. This happens when you get caught in a cycle in which you're constantly presenting options.

You show them the application workflow. They don't like it. They can't tell you why they don't like it, so they say, "Try using fewer screens."

You go back to your office, labor for a few days, and come back with the application redesigned with a new workflow. They don't like that either. They suggest, "A couple more screens might make it better."

Every developer dreads this process, and I would argue that it's the main reason we shy away from getting users involved. No one wants to build something by committee, so we allow users to get involved but severely limit the scope of what they can help us with.

We build an almost finished prototype and ask users about small minute features. By limiting their choice, we've effectively limited their involvement. It's phantom user-centered design. It's more lip service than reality. Hollis explains how we make this mistake:

> You've asked users for help—they're gonna give you help. But you didn't give them any room to give you help. You didn't give them any choices. You didn't give them any place to exert significant value judgment about what you're doing. You gave them this very narrow tunnel to be in and said, "Now, give me help in that small, confined space!"

Our job is to come up with choices and show the user possibilities. We do this to help them explore and communicate what they're looking for. The bottom line is that users can't do this effectively without seeing and visualizing multiple options or possibilities. We have to challenge ourselves to place different concepts and ideas in front of our users so we can drive to the core of what they need.

One strategy I employ is to put a challenging mockup in front of my users. Perhaps it's something that I know is radically different from what they'd be comfortable with. I'm not expecting them to love the design. In fact I'm hoping they hate it! I find users tend to be more articulate explaining what they don't like.

By listening to them list what they don't like, I can drill down to the heart of what my users need. It's a great strategy when you have fence sitters who can't seem to decide what they want. Try showing them a prototype that they're not expecting, and if they don't like it, ask why. You may be surprised how many design decisions can be made this way.

If you want to get your users out of the minutia of picking apart small details in your application, give them larger details to critique. Get them involved early and let them give you suggestions about the big stuff. Not only will you protect yourself from heading in the wrong direction, but your users will also feel more invested in the finished product.

A/B Testing

Even with viable data from direct user feedback, it may still be difficult to make a definitive design decision. Perhaps you're laboring over the old, "Should we go with this? Or should we go with that?" decision. In situations where both design decisions have merit or positive responses from users, you may consider conducting an *A/B test*.

A/B testing is the practice of testing users on two different designs and letting the data make the decision.

Let's say you're trying to decide where to display the Buy Now button on your product pages. Some people on your team think it should be directly below the product's picture, and others think that it should be placed beneath the product's description. Both seem like good ideas.

In this case, your A/B test would provide two different product pages for two separate groups of users. It would be a blind study because users would be unaware that there are actually two different experiences when purchasing a product.

In an A/B test, the winning design might be the configuration that causes users to click the Buy Now button more often. Essentially, we've relegated the design decision to a data decision. We're having users decide with their mouse-clicks which method is the most appropriate.

I guarantee that if you spend any amount of time on the Internet, you've participated in this type of A/B testing. Microsoft's Bing search service, for instance, uses A/B testing quite often. It's my default search engine, and many times I've noticed little changes here and there. Once I noticed that Bing changed the Search button from a magnifying glass to a button that read "Search," similar to the illustration shown in Figure 8-4. Later that day, it was switched back to the magnifying glass. Granted, the change was subtle, but now that I'm aware of A/B testing practices, I tend to pick up on those changes. Be observant and you may notice your favorite websites doing this, too!

Figure 8-4. Major websites like Bing employ A/B testing to observe the effects of subtle changes in usability

While A/B testing can be a great method to reach design decisions, it should be used in moderation. It can be easy to get into the practice of creating an A/B test for every facet of your application. By relying solely on data to make decisions, you focus less on understanding your users' behaviors.

Jeff Atwood, author of the blog Coding Horror, likens the challenges of A/B testing to the movie *Groundhog Day*. The movie, if you're unfamiliar with it, stars Bill Murray as a meteorologist named Phil who inexplicably ends up repeating the same day over and over. Phil uses this weird circumstance to go on thousands of dates with Rita, the woman he's fallen in love with. Much like A/B testing, with each date, Phil captures tiny details of Rita's likes and dislikes and makes different choices in every subsequent date. Over time, Phil uses all the data he's collected to create a seemingly perfect date. When Rita still doesn't fall in love with Phil, we realize that his idea just doesn't work.

Atwood explains:

> Phil wasn't making these choices because he honestly believed in them. He was making these choices because he wanted a specific outcome—winning over Rita—and the experimental data told him which path he should take. Although the date was technically perfect, it didn't ring true to Rita, and that made all the difference.

If you plan to try A/B testing, be mindful to not focus on irrelevant details. It's OK to test minutiae, but make sure you're considering the bigger picture as well.

Also note that proper A/B testing can require a large sample size to gather meaningful data.

In addition, the success of A/B testing relies on your ability to choose the right indicators. For example, if you're judging the success of your site's design by the color of a shopping cart icon, you may be missing more meaningful criteria, such as the ability for shoppers to find what items to buy.

The Short Version

- There's no magic number for how many study participants you should have. Although some disagree, Jakob Nielsen, a leading usability expert, suggests no more than five.

- Surveys can help you quickly collect feedback from many users. Surveys are relatively easy to distribute but often provide broad results.

- The Likert scale is a format of questions and answers used on surveys. The responses help subjects communicate value for things like frequency, importance, and satisfaction.

- One challenge with the Likert scale is acquiescence bias, which is the tendency for respondents to be agreeable or answer questions in a way they believe the surveyor would prefer.

- Conducting interviews requires more time, but is a great way to get direct user feedback. There are three types of interviews: unstructured (informal), structured (formal), and contextual (contextual inquiry).

- Unstructured interviews encourage conversation. They tend to be open-ended, without a specific agenda in mind. These types of interviews are used when you're beginning to explore the problem space.

- Structured interviews focus on consistency. It's recommended that you use a script and ask respondents questions in the same tone, order, and language.

- Contextual inquiries are much like interviews except that they focus on visiting and talking with users in their environment. By exploring the environment, you may uncover factors that affect your application, such as noise, lighting, distractions, etc.

- Task analysis is the thorough examination of a task or process. It's ideal that you actually observe the user completing the task; however, it's not required.

- Heuristic evaluation is the process of reviewing your application against industry standards and principles. Many software companies provide usability guidelines and will often block applications from their marketplace if these standards aren't met.

- Storyboards are a way to sketch the user experience step by step. Storyboards should give you an overall impression of how your application will flow.

- Prototypes can be a powerful tool in allowing users to visualize what you intend to build for them. Give your users choices and allow them to make decisions on larger aspects of your application.

- A/B testing is the process of presenting two interfaces to users and choosing the winning design based on the interface that provides the desired action. Decisions are made completely on data.

CHAPTER 9

Usability Studies

"People's minds are changed through observation
and not through argument."

—Will Rogers

Throughout this book I've made a case for the value of involving users in your design. In the previous chapter, we talked about different ways you can collect feedback and receive a broad understanding of the problem space. But what if you've already developed an application? How do you know if it's effectively meeting your users' needs?

Of course, you could always just ask them. We've talked a lot about having discussions with users and asking them questions; that process is still important. Users can tell us a lot about what's working and what's not. However, the most powerful way to gain insight into what a user needs is by directly observing them.

There are times when users' perspectives are skewed and subjective. Try asking users how long it takes for your application to load and you may get a variety of answers. For some users, your application's load time is just fine; for others it's painfully slow and unusable. Usability studies could help you determine just how long your application takes to load and, more importantly, how much of an impact it presents for your users. Usability testing quantifies your observations.

In fact, usability studies are one of the key features of user-centered design. If you're embarking on a website redesign, for instance, how do you know if your new design is better than the original? How do you know if you've actually achieved your vision and improved your users' experience?

Usability studies can help provide these answers. They establish baselines to track improvement in your application's design. By actively observing users and documenting their comments, actions, mistakes, and successes, you gain a valuable perspective on exactly how your application is being used.

What Are Usability Studies?

A usability study, or user testing, is the measured observation of users' behavior as they engage in the use of your software application. It's scientific in practice and favors metrics, measurements, and data to prove assumptions. There are two ways you can approach usability studies.

You can choose to complete the study in the user's environment. For instance, if you're building a call management application, you may elect to observe users in a live call center. This is referred to as a natural setting or an in-the-wild study. Much like the contextual inquiries we discussed in the previous chapter, usability studies are even more focused, systematic, and consistent.

The overall goal of a usability study is to measure the effectiveness of a feature or set of features within your application. To do this, you establish metrics such as time to complete or number of errors or a combination of these measurements. The study can also be combined with a survey to measure things that are difficult to observe like satisfaction or perception of value.

To complete a usability study successfully, you'll want to have a plan.

Creating a Testing Plan

It may seem obvious, but before you can conduct testing, you'll need to know what you're looking for. If you're building a mobile phone application, don't just hand the phone to someone and see if they like it. You'd be better served by a measured and organized approach. You'll want to have the right subjects, a prepared script, and a set of guidelines. These ensure that the data you collect is consistent and viable.

Just like creating surveys, it's important that you have the proper selection of users. If you're building a line-of-business application for a specific group of users, you'll obviously want to include them in your research. If you're building a mobile phone application for novice and experienced users, then you'll want to make sure you're including people from all levels of experience and familiarity. As we discussed with questionnaires, make sure to avoid *selection bias*, selecting users who are misrepresentative of the group.

A script can be a useful way to achieve consistency in your testing. It's easy to veer off course or become distracted when conducting a study. Preparing a script will allow you to deliver the test exactly the same way to each subject.

It may feel odd to read from a script, but it truly is the best way to ensure consistency. I find that a script sets the tone for a good quality study. Users will know that you're serious about getting valid results and you've come prepared for the study. If you need an example of what a script might look like, be sure to check out Appendix A at the end of this book.

Here are some things you should include in your script:

Introduction

Make sure you introduce the concept of the study and its purpose. Depending on the situation, you may need to ask for a legal release from the subject. Be sure that you're up-front about how you plan to use the results, especially if you plan to publish your findings.

Reassurance

Some subjects tend to be a bit nervous. Reassure them by explaining that you're testing the application and not them. If you're testing users within your organization, it's critical that you explain that the results will be anonymous.

No employee wants his boss to know he's having difficulty using the company's software. I find that using words like *test* or *grading* can rattle nerves; instead, you might consider using words like *observe* and *study*.

Testing Guidelines

Guidelines help define how the study will be conducted. Are you going to train subjects first? Are they allowed to ask questions? How much time do they have? Having these guidelines or rules in place will help subjects know what's expected of them and allow you to observe users consistently.

Tasks

Tasks will be the basis of your usability study. They are the metrics you plan to measure. For instance, you might decide to measure the time it takes for a user to change his profile picture or search for an item. You might also measure the number of queries required to locate a certain pair of shoes on a shopping site. Whatever the task or tasks are, make sure they're quantifiable.

Conclusion

Make sure you leave time at the end of the study to go over any questions or concerns. I've found that it can be fun to go over my observations with the subject. No matter how many times you told them that it wasn't a test, they still have this urge to know how they did.

Also, by sharing your observations, you may receive additional comments or explanations from the subject. Conversations after a study can clarify what you've just observed.

Thanks

Finally, be sure to thank your subjects. It's easy to get so wrapped up in observations and discussions that you forget this simple courtesy. Also, it might be a good idea to remind them of how you're planning on using the results and shore up any last-minute questions.

If appropriate, you might consider giving a small gift in appreciation of their time. I find coffee house gift cards work wonders!

What You'll Need

You may be wondering how many people should participate to have an effective study. One option is to apply Jakob Nielsen's no-more-than-five rule described in the previous chapter. Remember, the only guarantee is that if you don't do any studies, you can expect to discover *zero* usability problems. I would rather conduct a study with three people than not have any study at all. On the other side, having *too many* subjects can be a logistical nightmare that complicates and delays your efforts.

Don't think that testing a handful of people is a waste of time. If you only have access to a small group of users, I still encourage you to try usability testing. I've conducted very small studies and still gained valuable insights.

Other than the number of participants, here are some other things you should have while preparing for a study:

Stopwatch

If you're planning on measuring how long it takes subjects to complete a task to determine the success of your design, you'll want to use a stopwatch or one of the many smartphone applications with stopwatch features. Obviously, time to complete should not rule all design decisions. Just because a user can complete a task quickly doesn't mean that the design is more enjoyable. Even if it isn't a specific factor in my design decision, I like to keep track of the time each subject spends completing tasks.

Notepad

Use a notepad and pen, even though it might be tempting to take notes on a laptop or mobile device. Users move and talk quickly, and you'll want to be prepared to capture any behavior or comment as it happens. I find that a quickly drawn symbol or diagram can be a more effective way to capture my observations. Pen and paper afford me that flexibility.

Environment

Consider the environment that best complements what you are trying to study. If it's important that there are minimal distractions, you may want to secure a location that is out of the way or quiet. Make sure you've prepared the location for your study. Basic things like comfortable chairs, lighting, network connectivity, and room temperature all affect your study. Be sure to check the environment and tools your subjects will be using to ensure they won't interfere or become a distraction. Subjects will appreciate that you've prepared the space for their study. If you plan on spending a significant amount of time with them, make sure to have water and snacks available.

Spreadsheet or Database

Tabulate your data in a spreadsheet or database. If time permits, you may want to build your own mini-application to collect it. Having data organized electronically will help you with quickly identifying patterns. Microsoft Access and Excel are both great products for this kind of data aggregation and reporting.

Again, users move quickly. There will be little time to input data while observing behaviors. I recommend collecting your findings on your notepad first then entering them into a spreadsheet or database later.

Cameras or Audio Recording

Employ video cameras or audio-recording equipment to capture all respondents' comments and behavior. Typically, I'm not a fan of this equipment because it tends to distract the subject. Most folks hate the idea of being on camera, and no matter how much you reassure them to the contrary, subjects will feel like they are being tested. Having a camera pointed at their face doesn't help quell that anxiety.

If you feel that a camera or recording device is necessary, make sure that the equipment is unobtrusive. Also, include the fact that you will be recording the study in your script. You may also want to consider giving your subject the courtesy of opting out of the recording.

Using your smartphone camera to take a few pictures might be less intrusive. Sometimes a gallery of photos is enough to document how subjects responded during the study.

I realize that to some of you this level of preparation might seem daunting, and the idea of writing a script might seem a little overboard. You may be tempted to just sit down with your users and watch them use your application. I can't stress enough how important it is to have a plan for your usability study. Much like the entire user-centered design process, having a vision and documented plan for your usability studies are the best way to ensure you receive meaningful results.

Conducting the Study

After you put a plan in place, it will be time to conduct your study. I recommend printing each task you plan to study on its own piece of paper. If you place a packet of instructions in front of subjects, there's a good chance they'll begin to leaf through it and get ahead of themselves. Having the tasks printed individually minimizes those distractions and prevents your subjects from skipping ahead.

Additionally, you'll want to have a printed copy of your script for you to read. Prepare the script to coincide with each task. Ideally, you'll have an overall script for the study and mini-scripts for each task. Make sure the language is consistent from task to task, even if it feels like you're repeating yourself.

One thing that you want to continually remind subjects to do is to think aloud. This is the process of the subject telling you what she's thinking while she completes the task. It's all too easy for users to quietly focus on completing the task. The problem with that is that you're missing out on their thought process. You can't really tell what's going through their head as they use your application unless they tell you.

Your script should include the instruction to talk aloud several times. You may consider giving this instruction before the start of every task. Most subjects will resist because it feels silly—they'll feel like they're rambling—but encourage them to anyway. Their stream of consciousness will be full of insight, even if they don't realize.

Imagine that the user is looking for the Search button in your application. If she doesn't say, "OK, I'm looking for the search button now," there's no way for you to connect with what she's trying to do. By having subjects think aloud, you can better document their actions and hone in on what might be tripping them up. Let's say you're testing an email and calendar application. A great usability study should have your subjects sounding like this:

> OK, I need to send a message. I'm going to click on this button because it says New.

> Oh, wait. That looks like that opened a new appointment. I don't want that. How do I close it? Oh, there it is.

> All right, I get it now. I need to select the Inbox first. That's weird though; I wish the icons were different so I could tell between the two.

In this case we would document that the user was having trouble decoding the difference between creating a new message and a new appointment. This will remind us to review how we're handling the creation of new items in our application. Perhaps it will drive us to consider a new design decision. If the user hadn't mentioned that she was trying to create a new message, we might've missed that she was having trouble.

If a user has questions about how to complete a task, I strongly suggest that you only clarify what the task requires. Limit your instruction and do your best to eliminate any training while the user is trying to complete the task. You want the subject to try and figure it out for herself and think aloud as she does.

Too often, usability studies end up turning into training sessions. There's nothing wrong with showing the user how to complete tasks, just make sure this training doesn't occur *during* the study. If your application requires training (e.g., a complex line-of-business application that users have never seen before), then consider doing training before the study. If possible, have enough time between training and the study so that users are able to recall how the application works.

If subjects ask for help, rather than telling them what to do, consider flipping the question around:

Subject: "So, I need to find a way to print this out. Is this the right way to do it?"

Me: "How do you think you should be able to do it?"

Subject: "Well, other programs have the Print feature under the File menu, but this application doesn't have it there."

By responding to the subject with a question, I was tipped off to the fact that I should consider putting the Print function where other applications place it (under the File menu). Avoid the temptation to provide training to increase your chances of catching things you might've missed.

If it's possible, position yourself behind subjects. I find that it's much easier to take notes and make observations without distracting them.

When each task is complete, take a moment to capture your measurements (elapsed time, number of errors, etc.). Consider giving subjects a small questionnaire while you jot down these last minute notes. I've found this to be a smooth rhythm that doesn't make subjects wait while you're furiously writing in your notebook. Also, while they're completing the questionnaire, you can prepare for the next task (reset the stopwatch, get the next printed instructions, and so on).

The questionnaire could be satisfaction-based, with questions about users' experience while completing the task. See Chapter 7 for more information about conducting surveys.

Things happen quickly during a usability test. You'll be surprised by how many observations and off-handed comments you'll want to write down for review. Having a clear script, printed materials, and any other tools ready to go will keep your study moving efficiently.

Don't Hesitate to Practice

If you're eager to get out there and begin, that's great! However, I encourage you to fight the temptation to prematurely study your users. A great way to test the script and structure of your study is to practice. Consider asking a friend or colleague to run through the entire study with you. This will give you an opportunity to find any typos or confusing language in your script.

Ideally, you'll find someone who is a good candidate for your application. If you practice with a fellow project member, he may be too familiar with the application to point out confusing areas.

Regardless of whom you find, spend time practicing to be prepared to conduct the official study.

Compiling Your Findings

Your usability studies should provide you with a trove of insight and feedback. It may be tempting to take one comment and start making design modifications, but you'll be better served by taking the time to compile all your findings. By calculating your measurements and organizing your comments, you'll convert the data into meaningful conclusions. The data from your usability studies can help you justify your design decisions, especially when there's conflict among team members about how the application should function.

Here's an example. While studying a redesign of our corporate intranet, I discovered that it was significantly less efficient for users to navigate a list of items rather than searching for a specific item. During this study, we examined our employee directory, which gave users the ability to search for an employee and see a list of employees by selecting a letter of the last name, as shown in Figure 9-1.

Figure 9-1. Our original employee directory provided users with a list of employees and the ability to search for someone

When asked to locate a specific employee, more than 90% of employees clicked to view a list of all employees with the shared letter of the last name. This would require them to scan a lengthy list. Some users took more than four minutes before locating the employee they were looking for.

When I asked why they chose to view a list of all the employees rather than using the available Search box, I received a common response: they were concerned they would spell the employee's name wrong. They believed that it would be better to scan the entire list of all employees rather than take a risk of entering the name incorrectly.

The study helped me realize that if given the choice between searching and viewing a list of results, our staff did not feel confident in using Search, even though it would've been a far more efficient option. Primarily, their concern was spelling an employee's name wrong.

Misspelling a name was a legitimate issue. Employees have unique spellings and long last names. It could take several queries to get the name you were looking for.

Therefore, I decided to build suggestions into our search, as depicted in Figure 9-2. I realized that we already had the list of employee names. Why not create a way to suggest all the possible employees as the user was typing his query? This would reduce errors and give users confidence to rely on a search engine rather than scanning lengthy lists.

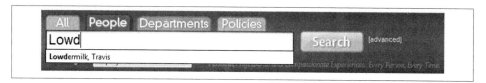

Figure 9-2. Revised employee search using suggestions

As with any change, I experienced pushback from some staff and leaders. They were adamant that reviewing the lists was easier than typing an employee's name. However, their disagreement was merely anecdotal compared to my data.

I was able to prove that the average user spends 21 minutes a year looking for employees. At over 3,500 employees being paid an average rate of $20.50 an hour, that was an estimated expense of $25,000 a year! Admittedly, this isn't very sturdy math (in fact this is about as fuzzy as it gets), but the point is that having measurements allowed me to prove to the naysayers that their assumptions were incorrect.

This is why usability studies are the crux of the user-centered design methodology— they correct assumptions through the systematic observation of users and collection of their feedback. There's no going with your gut in the user-centered design world.

I'm confident that when you begin usability studies, not only will you strengthen your relationship with users, but you'll also be a better programmer. You'll learn what works, what doesn't, and most importantly, you'll have the data to back it up.

The Short Version

- A usability study is the process of testing your application's design by observing users, measuring their performance, and documenting their comments.

- Just like in the entire user-centered design process, make sure your usability study is thoughtfully planned. You'll want to know what tasks you're testing and how you plan to measure them.

- Prepare a written script. This will ensure that the way you interact with each subject is consistent and on track.

- While users complete the task, encourage them to think aloud. This will help you understand their thought process and enable you to pick up on things your application might've missed.

- You'll want to be prepared with a stopwatch, notepad, acceptable location, and a collection of subjects who best represent your target users.

- When conducting the study, sit behind the user so you won't distract her with your note taking. After each task, consider giving out a questionnaire so you can finish last-minute documentation and prepare for the next task.

- Practicing is a great way to make sure you've prepared a study that will give you the best results.

- After you've received study results, calculate your measurements and organize your comments. The data will help justify your design decisions.

CHAPTER 10

You're Never Finished

"Here is the test to find whether your mission on earth is finished. If you're alive, it isn't."

—Richard Bach

My hope is that our time together has helped you understand the value of putting users in the center of your development process. I realize user-centered design is not easy and requires a great deal of investment on your part. However, I strongly believe that it's worth the investment.

When you begin to work in step with users, you save yourself valuable time by heading in the right direction. I don't know about you, but I hate having to rewrite code or throw away an hour's worth of work. I feel silly when I put my application in front of the user and realize I've missed something obvious, which renders the application unusable. It only takes of few situations like these to make you realize that you can't build applications without users' help.

However, I'm not going to suggest that the user-centered design process is the quickest methodology for getting your application out the door. You'll still make mistakes, even when users tell you exactly what they need. Guess what? Users change their minds all the time! They ask for one thing, see it, and decide they want something else.

This is why it's important to not only listen to their needs, but also observe them to get a holistic view of the problem space.

With all that said, one of the most important aspects of user-centered design is the willingness to get it right. You have to be willing to start over if necessary. After all, what good is testing your design if you're unwilling to change it based on the results? This requires you to check your ego to give your users the very best application you can build.

It's Impossible to Get It Right the First Time

As difficult as it can be, you must give up the fantasy that you'll get everything right in the first version of your application. You have to fight against becoming paralyzed because you're unwilling to release your application until you make everything perfect.

Strike the right balance between accepting that you're releasing an imperfect product and determining to get things right.

Jeff Weir explains this well:

> Only with iteration will your product, or whatever you create, actually get better. You're never going to get it right on the first try. *No one gets it right on the first try.* Otherwise, we'd still have the first iPod.

Having developed applications and websites for some time now, I can tell you that it's still difficult to hear criticism. As much as I pride myself on my thick skin, I still want to hear the user say, "It's perfect. You don't need to change *anything!*" To date, I don't think I've ever heard that, and I don't expect to any time soon.

A skill that I've crafted over many years is the ability to distance my personal value and self-worth from the outcome of my applications. At the risk of sounding like a psychologist, I'm going to state this again because it bears constant repeating.

We need to understand that if our design fails, it's not a *personal failure*. We have to explore what we've missed or the questions we might not have asked. If our design doesn't work, it's because we failed at getting the right information; it doesn't mean we failed at being a programmer and should consider another profession.

Having the right mindset will allow you to be less defensive when receiving feedback. It will also protect you from getting discouraged or feeling like a loser if you built something that users don't like.

Users can be demanding, but my experience has shown that when we include them in the development process, they have a better understanding of how to communicate what's missing. Additionally, they have a better understanding of what they're asking for.

Users that have worked with me in designing an application end up learning the difficulties and technical limitations. We need to acknowledge that just because our users don't have computer science degrees doesn't mean they aren't adept at helping us solve technical problems.

Be Prepared to Reboot

Developers have a tendency to be code hoarders, to fall in love with code and want to keep it forever. We leave it in our applications because we never know if we may need or want to repurpose it. Our applications become a virtual storage shed for all of our coding ideas.

Certainly, code repurposing has its merits, and there is no reason to reinvent the wheel for every project. However, it has its drawbacks. If we continually institute the same code for each project, we run the risk of implementing the same solution to every problem. It can become more difficult to provide new solutions to usability concerns. We end up sizing up each user request as an exercise to prove that "we've got code for that."

If our application doesn't meet users' needs, we need to ask basic questions:

- What are we trying to achieve?
- How are we providing value?
- What do our users love?
- What do our users hate?

The immense challenge of building an application makes it easy to drift from these questions. Still, building a great application may mean we have to go back to the beginning. It may mean we have to start over and revisit our vision. We might have to reboot our assumptions.

I know how hard it is to throw away code. I know you're thinking, "This code took me months to figure out! Now you want me to throw it all away because my users don't need it?"

Yes. That's exactly what I want you to do.

When we put our code before our users, we move away from the vision we had in the first place. Our job is to make great applications, not great code. If your code doesn't support your vision for the application, then it needs to go. It's as simple as that.

Challenge yourself and your team to revisit your project's vision. Continually take time out of your development cycle to ensure that you're heading in the right direction. Make sure that the choices you've made are best for your users and not because you're afraid to delete code.

Be bold and willing to re-evaluate assumptions to make sure they still have merit in the light of new discoveries.

This is why it's so important to have a team mission statement or manifesto for your project. By having a clear definition of what you're trying to achieve, you save yourself the time of getting off track. Revisit your mission statement often, and don't hesitate to use it while making difficult design decisions.

Final Thoughts

I'd like to make one final point before we conclude. Some of us developers tend to be an egotistical bunch. There's a level of self-importance and power that comes with creating applications that users rely on. With a mouse click or stroke of the keyboard, we can change everything!

On the flip side, many of us have an incredible pressure to be experts and have it all figured out. Many times, we find ourselves alone, and it's easy to get disillusioned or frustrated. In short time, your users become the *enemy*. They represent the riotous horde just outside your door chanting, "When will it be done?"

Take a deep breath; user-centered design requires soft skills. You have to patiently listen to your users and genuinely desire their feedback. I'm not saying you have to *agree* with what they're saying, but you should, at the very least, value it. Remember that at the end of the day, our users have a lot to teach us.

I've had users give me suggestions that are so embarrassingly simple that I don't know how I missed them. After all, I'm supposed to be the expert! The reality is that it's impossible for me to see everything. Developing applications requires such an intense focus on the smallest details that I have to concede my ability to catch and think of everything.

To do it right requires help, and there's no better group of people to help us than the users themselves.

That's the beauty of the user-centered design approach. It protects us from the failed curtain unveiling, the point where we unveil our application to a dissatisfied group of users. It gives us a roadmap that maintains our empathy for users by continually focusing on their experience.

What I've offered in this book is a quick introduction. There is a wealth of knowledge in the usability and user-experience worlds. Follow the experts and learn from them. If you need help finding some experts, see the section Chapter 11.

Encourage your own creativity by taking time to explore new things. Create a plan to help you implement your user-centered design strategy. Gather feedback from your users and ask them specific questions about the problem space. Create prototypes to test early design considerations, and let your users evaluate them.

Finally, conduct detailed and organized usability studies. Measure your application's usability by observing users as they try to complete tasks. Document their comments and use data to support your design decisions.

Implement the user-centered design methodology outlined in this book, and you'll pursue the very best for your users. When users know they're at the center of your application's focus, they'll continue to reward it with their preference and loyalty.

CHAPTER 11

Other Resources

In this book, I've written a lot about encouraging your creativity by following experts in the field. This section represents some of the best resources and tools I've found. If you find some that are missing, please email me at *books@travislowdermilk.com*.

Twitter

Twitter is an invaluable resource for all the latest happenings in the usability and user-experience (UX) world. Consider opening a Twitter account to follow these great resources:

Aarron Walter @aarron
> Director of UX at MailChimp and author of *Designing for Emotion* (A Book Apart).

A Book Apart @abookapart
> Publisher of some really great design and web development books. These books inspired me to write this one!

Dan Cederholm @simplebits
> Co-founder of Dribbble, an online show-and-tell for designers, and SimpleBits LLC web design studio. Dan is an extremely talented designer and offers a great deal of insight into the world of usability and design.

Design Observer @designobserver
> The group hosts an expansive website about the world of design (*http://www.design observer.com*). They also produce an incredible podcast series called "Design Matters," hosted by Debbie Millman.

EffectiveUI @effectiveui
> User-experience design agency based in Denver, Colorado, that uses Twitter to help folks stay abreast of leading design trends and shifts in the industry. It's also behind

the book *Effective UI* (O'Reilly), which I used to prepare the section on usability studies.

Human Factors International @humanfactors
A world leader in user-centered design that keeps you plugged into emerging trends with supportive articles.

Luke Wroblewski @lukew
An internationally recognized digital product leader and author of *Mobile First* (A Book Apart), which makes the case that websites should be designed to be considerate of mobile devices.

Measuring Usability @MeasuringU
Jeff Sauro is the author of *Quantifying the User Experience: Practical Statistics of User Research* (Morgan Kaufmann) and founder of Measuring Usability, a research firm that helps companies quantify their user experience.

Nick Campbell @nickvegas
Campbell is a funny and amazingly talented designer. He hosts a motion design website as well as a general design podcast called Greyscalegorilla (*http://www.grey scalegorilla.com*).

Nielsen Norman Group @NNgroup
Founded by Jakob Nielson and Don Norman, this group is the leading agency in usability and user-centered design.

Roman Mars @romanmars
Roman is the host of 99% Invisible (*http://www.99percentinvisible.org*), an absolutely fantastic podcast series on design.

Typographica.org @typographica
Editor Stephen Coles on fonts and typography.

User Interface Engineering @UIE
A leading research, training, and consulting firm that specialized in UX and website and product usability. It has great suggestions from the entire spectrum of usability concerns.

UX Magazine @uxmag
An online publication about the complex field of user experience. It's comprised of very talented writers who produce thought-provoking and engaging articles.

Tools for Prototyping

There are many prototyping applications available to you, but these two seem to be the industry standards at the moment:

Balsamiq Mockups

With a focus on agility, Balsamiq (*http://www.balsamiq.com*) is a great tool to communicate early mockups, layouts, and design. Balsamiq uses a hand-drawn effect for all of its widgets, which creates an experience that feels conceptual and iterative.

Axure RP Pro

Axure RP Pro (*http://www.axure.com*) provides a great deal of sophistication for a prototyping tool. Axure allows you to use widgets, and by adjusting their sketchiness, you can quickly change the fidelity of your prototype. Additionally, Axure RP Pro provides robust events and conditional framework so that you can set basic actions to occur in response to clicks and key presses.

Websites

alistapart.com

A magazine that explores design, content strategy, development, standards, and practices. The primary focus is on web development.

abookapart.com

Created by the folks at *A List Apart*, A Book Apart has published a collection of books that focus on topics like HTML5, CSS, content strategy, and more. The best thing about these books is their size and informal tone. They are easy to read and fun!

boxesandarrows.com

Devoted to the practice and discussion of design, interaction design, information architecture, and the business of design.

netmagazine.com

.net is a magazine for web designers and developers. Topics range from tutorials on the latest design trends to interviews with the Web's biggest designers.

smashingmagazine.com

One of the world's leading online publishing companies in the field of web design and web development. This website is a culmination of daily articles and tips from leading experts in the UX design industry.

useit.com/alertbox

Authored by Jakob Nielsen, one of the foremost experts in the field of usability and user experience. The site is full of articles with his opinions on the latest design trends. If you want to be where the usability discussion begins, this is the place to be.

uxmatters.com

Provides insights and inspiration to professionals at every level as they journey through the world of user experience.

Sample Project Template

Template

We refer to our template as a Software Development Life Cycle (SDLC). This does not reflect an all-encompassing SDLC. Many firms have more elaborate development processes and documentation. As with all recommendations in this book, this template should be used as a starting point that you should change to fit your needs.

Project Title

Software Development Life Cycle Project Template

Mission Statement

Software Development Life Cycle Summary

The intent of this document is to collect, define, and organize project details and requirements. The template is designed to be iterative, meaning that it will evolve over the life of the project.

The template includes the following key sections:

1. **Project Details**: These include the summary of the project. They're designed to collect the following information:

2. **Title**: The title or codename of the project.

3. **Description**: A summary defining the objective of the project.

4. **Stakeholders**: Members who are involved with or have requested the project.

5. **Impact Assessment**: The observed or intended impact of the project deliverable: Who will be affected by this project? How many users? What business processes will be changed as a result of this project?

6. **User Requirements**: The requirements of the project, as specified by the user. The user requirements section includes a signature of agreement. As requirements evolve, many iterations of the user requirements sheet may be included.

7. **Specifications Sheet (Functional Requirements)**: The technical details of the project, or the deliverables that will be developed and/or designed to meet the user requirements.

8. **Data Models**: Data Flow Diagrams and/or Data Structure Diagrams.

9. **Data Processes**: These are data processes or scripts that the project depends on. The list includes the process name; a description of where it's located, what it does, etc.; and runtime/duration. This table will be updated throughout the life of the product.

10. **Prototypes**: Copies of low- or high-fidelity screenshots, mockups, models, etc.

11. **Maintenance Notes**: Additional notes that would be pertinent to the support of this product.

Project Details

Fill out the various details below to outline your project. If changes are made, use Strikethrough and provide a date when the change was made. Then you can append the revised title, description, etc.

IMPORTANT: Do not delete values, as they are the official record of development for the project!

Title

Title of the project or product

Description

Description of the project or product

Name(s) of Stakeholder(s)

Names of key stakeholders

Impact Assessment

A summary of the impact of the project/product

User Requirements

Fill out the various user requirements below. If changes are made, use Strikethrough and provide a date when the change was made. Then you can append the new or revised user requirement.

IMPORTANT: Do not delete user requirements, as they are the official record of development on the project!

	User requirement	Description	Requestor name
1			
2			
3			
4			
5			

I agree that these user requirements meet the needs of my request. If changes occur to the user requirements, I will notify the developer with a new request. I understand that making changes to these user requirements could institute a delay in the projected delivery time of the project.

_____

Signature of Key Stakeholder   Date

Specifications Sheet (Functional Requirements)

Fill out the various user requirements below. If changes are made, use Strikethrough and provide a date when the change was made. Then you can append the new or revised functional requirement.

IMPORTANT: Do not delete functional requirements, as they are the official record of development on the project!

	Functional requirement	Description	Meets user req. #
1			
2			
3			
4			
5			

I agree that these functional requirements meet the needs of my request. If changes occur to the functional requirements, I will notify the developer with a new request. I understand that making changes to these functional requirements could institute a delay in the projected delivery time of the project.

_____

Signature of Key Stakeholder   Date

Data and Workflow Models

Include diagrams showing data structure at a high level. The intent of this process is to document how the data is structured to support the project.

Data Processes

Process name	Description	Runtime/frequency
1		
2		
3		
4		
5		

Prototypes

Include low- and/or high-fidelity prototypes. You can include early sketches or screen-shots. The point of prototyping is that we give users an opportunity to review early conceptual models. It can be helpful to include even your earliest conceptual designs, so you can track the progression of your application.

Maintenance Notes

Include notes that will be required to provide support for your product. This part of the document should be updated throughout the life of the product. As support requirements change, amend this document with a date next to each entry.

Example Persona

Dan Welks

Age: 29

Status: Married, 1 child (2 years old)

Location: Austin, Texas

Occupation: Web Designer

Hobbies: Reading (mostly tech blogs), playing guitar, playing video games, and photography.

Favorite items: iPad, iPhone, vintage AM/FM radio, and the new SUV he and his wife just bought.

Needs: Dan has his iPad wherever he goes. He'd love a way to jot down notes or quickly sketch out a website design.

Currently, Dan will sketch ideas on printer paper or a dry-erase board. Sometimes, he'll take a picture of his drawings with his iPad, but it doesn't allow him to make changes later.

Dan wishes there was a way to keep all his notes and doodles in one place. He's tried carrying around a notebook and pen, but it's cumbersome while also carrying his iPad.

Beliefs: Dan has tried other drawing, sketching, and note-taking apps on his iPad. None of them has been very enjoyable. He does like Sketchbook Pro but finds the tools complex and daunting. He already has Photoshop, so if he wants to build something that detailed, he'll just use that.

Dan believes that the best way to draw and take notes is with pen and paper. He thinks drawing with an iPad app lacks agility and feels very unnatural.

Sample Script for a Usability Study

 This is a script template for a usability study and is intended to help you get started. Obviously, the tasks and focus of your study will be determined by you. However, this template will give you an idea of the language and organization of a script. After the introduction, you can create a similar script for each task.

Essentially, each script should have the same tone and language of the introduction. The only difference is that it will have specific instructions of tasks you'll be observing.

Introduction to Study

Thank you for agreeing to participate in the testing of *name of app*, an application that allows you to *short description of the application.*

Today, we're going to be testing three main features of the application:

- *Feature*
- *Feature*
- *Feature*

The study should take *estimated time* to complete.

The first task will require you to *short description of first task*. Next, you will be asked to *short description of second task*. Finally, I'll observe you *short description of third task*.

Prior to each task, I will outline the specific goals of the task to you. Each task will begin when I say, "Begin task" and complete when I say, "End task." I will not be able to answer specific questions during the task; however, I can clarify any instructions. Before we begin each task, I will ask you if you have any questions about the instructions.

Please narrate your thought process by thinking aloud. For instance, if you were going to *appropriate action*, you would say out loud, "I'm going to *appropriate action*." This will help me understand what you're trying to do and improve the effectiveness of this study.

Please remember that we are not testing you in this study. We are only testing the application's ability to help you in completing your task. All notes, documentation, and comments will be completely anonymous.

References

Steve Jobs quote on focus groups
> *Bloomberg Business Week* May 12, 1998. Steve Jobs on Apple's Resurgence: "Not a One-Man Show." *http://buswk.co/Yf7HCQ.*

Steve Jobs quote on intersection of liberal arts and technology
> Jobs, Steve. January 27, 2010. Apple iPad Keynote. San Francisco, CA.

What Is Usability?, Collecting User Requirements, Creating Functional Requirements, Feedback Principle, Consistency, Fitt's Law, Studying Users, Likert Scales, What Are Usability Studies?
> Rogers, Yvonne, Helen Sharp, and Jenny Preece. 2011. *Interaction design: Beyond human-computer interaction.* 3rd Ed. Wiley, Print.

Usability Is Not a Waste of Time (or Money), Using Prototypes
> Hollis, Billy. June 21, 2012. Personal Interview.

> Lund, Arnold M. May/June 1997. "Another approach to justifying the cost of usability." *Interactions.*

Knowing When to Listen to Your Users (and When Not To), The "Control Freak"
> Goodman, Elizabeth, Mike Kuniavsky, and Andrea Moed. 2012. *Observing the user experience: A practitioner's guide to user research.* Waltham: Morgan Kaufmann.

Dealing with Different Types of Users: The "Devil's Advocate"
> Kelley, Tom, and Jonathan Littman. 2005. *The ten faces of innovation: IDEO's strategies for beating the devil's advocate and driving creativity throughout your organization.* DOUBLEDAY.

Dealing with Negativity and the Attribution Error
> Heath, Chip, and Dan Heath. 2010. *Switch: How to change things when change is hard.* Broadway Books.

Having a Plan
Anderson, Jonathan, John McRee, Robb Wilson and the EffectiveUI Team. 2010. *Effective UI.* Cambridge: O'Reilly Media, Inc.

Documenting Prototypes
Fitzpatrick, Brian W., and Ben Collins-Sussman. 2012. *Team geek: A software developer's guide to working well with others.* Cambridge: O'Reilly Media, Inc.

Creating a Personal Manifesto
Ingebretsen, Robby. April 14, 2012. "Paper, manifestos and why you need one to be great at anything." *http://nerdplusart.com/paper-manifestos-and-why-you-need-one-to-be-great-at-anything.*

Paper for the iPad by FiftyThree, Consistency
Hamburger, Ellis. March 29, 2012. "Paper: the next great iPad app, from the brains behind Courier." *The Verge. http://www.theverge.com/2012/3/29/2909537/paper-drawing-ipad-app-fiftythree-brains-behind-courier.*

Exercising Restraint
Buxton, Bill. January 12, 2007. "Multi-touch systems that I have known and loved." *http://www.billbuxton.com/multitouchOverview.html.*

Building a Narrative
Walker, Julian. May 1, 2012. Personal Interview.

Creativity Requires Courage (and Hard Work)
Hogan, Blaine. 2011. *Untitled: Thoughts on the creative process.* Alpharetta: Clark. *http://creativecollective.is/portfolio/untitled-thoughts-on-the-creative-process/.*

Steal (I Mean Borrow) From Others
Kleon, Austin. 2012, *Steal like an artist: 10 things nobody told you about being creative.* New York: Workman Publishing Company.

Heffron, Jack. 2003. *The writer's idea workshop: How to make your good ideas great.* Cincinnati: Writer's Digest Books.

Creativity Requires Questioning
Lehrer, Jonah. *Imagine: How creativity works.* Houghton Mifflin Harcourt Publishing Company. Electronic Book.

Pick Up a Pencil (source for Jeff Gothelf's talk at Agile UX NYC 2012)
Constable, Giff. February 29, 2012. "Increase collaboration through sketching." *http://giffconstable.com/2012/02/increase-collaboration-through-sketching/.*

Creative Freedom
Pink, Daniel H. 2009. *Drive: The surprising truth about what motivates us.* New York: Riverhead Books.

Understanding Your Goal

Weir, Jeff. May 20, 2012. Personal Interview.

Principle of Proximity (Gestalt Principle), Mental Models and Metaphors, Visibility Principle, and Hick's Law

Lidwell, William, Kritina Holden, and Jill Butler. 2003. *Universal principles of design: A cross-disciplinary reference.* Beverly: Rockport Publishers. *http://www.qbook shop.com/products/153021/9781592530076/Universal-Principles-of-Design.html.*

Affordance and Constraints

Norman, Donald A. 1988. *The design of everyday things.* Basic Book,. Electronic Book.

Hick's Law, Fitt's Law

Wickens, Christopher, John Lee, Yili Liu, and Sallie Gordon Becker. 2004. *An introduction to human factors engineering.* Pearson Education, Inc.

How Many Users Will I Need?

Nielsen, Jakob. March 19, 2000. "Why you only need to test with 5 users." *http://www.nngroup.com/articles/why-you-only-need-to-test-with-5-users/.*

Acquiescence Response Bias

Lavrakas, Paul J. 2008. Encyclopedia of Survey Research Methods. Sage Publications, Inc. Online reference. *http://bit.ly/10PorRi.*

A/B Testing

Christian, Brian. April 25, 2012. "The A/B test: Inside the technology that's changing the rules of business." *Wired Magazine. http://www.wired.com/business/2012/04/ff_abtesting/.*

Atwood, Jeff. January 20, 2010. "Groundhog Day, or, the problem with A/B testing." *Coding Horror: Programming and Human Factors. http://www.codinghorror.com/blog/2010/07/groundhog-day-or-the-problem-with-ab-testing.html.*

What Are Usability Studies?, Creating a Testing Plan, What You'll Need, Conducting the Study

Pernice, Kara, Amy Schade, and Jakob Nielsen. *Intranet Usability Guidelines, vol 1: Understanding and Studying Users (Test Data, User Behavior, and Methodolgy 2nd Edition).* Nielsen Norman Group. Electronic Document. *http://www.nngroup.com.*

Index

We'd like to hear your suggestions for improving our indexes. Send email to index@oreilly.com.

prototyping, 89
  tools for, 110
proximity principle, 63

Q

questions
  questionnaire for usability testing, 101
  survey questions using clear and neutral language, 82

R

Rapid Response Team (RRT) project (example), 30
reaction time, or RT, 74
references, 127–129
repetition of your understanding to users, 86
repurposing code, 107
Request for Proposal or Letter of Intent, 28
resources, other, 109–111
  prototyping tools, 110
  Twitter, 109
  websites, 111
restraint, exercising in number of features, 41
Ribbon interface, Microsoft Office, 64
Rice, Anne, 56
roles for users (or team members), 22
Ross, Lee, 24
RRT (Rapid Response Team) project (example), 30

S

scenarios
  creating for personas, 44
  using scenario-based questioning for task analysis, 86
screenshots of prototypes, 37
script for usability testing, 96
scripts for usabiity studies
  sample script, 124
SDLC (Software Development Life Cycle)
  sample project template, 113–122
search interface, DePaul University course catalog, 66
search results, 56
self-worth and personal value, distancing from outcome, 106
ShipIt Days, 53

sketching your ideas, 50
social networks
  finding people who personify users, 16
soft skills for UCD, 108
Software Development Life Cycle (SDLC), 28
  sample project template, 113–122
specifications sheet, 118
spreadsheet or database for usbaility testing, 99
stakeholders, identifying in project template, 32
status, 65
  indicating status of an application, 66
Steal Like an Artist: 10 Things Nobody Told You About Being Creative, 55
stopwatch for usability testing, 98
storyboarding, 87–89
structured interviews, 83
super users, level of engagement, 21
surveys, using to gather feedback, 81–83
Switch: How to Change Things When Change is Hard, 23

T

task analysis, 86
Team Geek, 37
team mission statement, creating, 30
The Ten Faces of Innovation, 22
three-pronged electrical plug, 72
title, project, 31
top box scoring, 82
training, usability studies and, 101
Twitter
  resources for usability and UX, 109
  search results, 56
typeface, 65

U

UCD (user-centered design), 2
  never finished, 105–108
    being prepared to reboot, 107
    impossibility of getting right first time, 106
  not a bug report, 10
  not a distraction, 11
  not a waste of money or time, 8
  not just design, 7
  not subjective, 7
  questions to ask first, 12

relationship between usabiity, HCI, UCD, and UX, 6
versus usability, 5
Undo, implementation in Paper, 71
unstructured interviews, 83
Untitled: Thoughts on the Creative Process, 50
usability
    defined, 5
    observing users and asking questions of them, 58
    problems found per number of users, 80
    relationship between HCI, UCD, UX and, 6
usability studies, 95–104
    compiling findings, 102–103
    conducting, 100–101
    creating testing plan, 96–98
    defined, 96
    necessities for, 98
    practicing for, 102
    sample script for, 124
user experience (see UX)
user requirements, 117
    collecting, 32
    connecting functional requirements to, 34
    user experience goals versus, 48
user testing (see usability studies)
user-centered design (see UCD)
users
    creating personas for, 43
    dealing with different types, 20–23
        control freak, 21
        devil's advocate, 22
        information overloader, 20
    knowing when to listen to users, 17–20
    negativity of, dealing with, 23
    no access to, 15–17
    number needed to gather feedback from, 79

selection for usability testing, 96
UX (user experience), 47
    (see also creativity and user experience)
    creativity and, 47
    defined, 6
    having user experience goals, 48
    relationship between usability, HCI, UCD and, 6

V

vending machine, dataflow diagram of, 36
Viscocity, 53
visibility, 65–67
    status of an application, 66
    visual feedback, 66
vision, 39
    (see also personal manifesto, creating)
    revisiting for a project, 107
visitor directory (example)
    auditory feedback, 84
    with animated dots leading to elevator, 18
visual hierarchy, 67

W

Walker, Julian, 42
websites, 111
Weir, Jeff, 53, 106
Windows applications, 87
workflow diagrams, 36, 119
    using task analysis for, 86
workflows
    illustrating with storyboarding, 88
    user, learning about, 20
The Writer's Idea Workshop, 56

About the Author

Travis Lowdermilk has been developing custom software experiences for over 15 years in industries ranging from architecture, business, and health care. Currently, he works for a community hospital in central California. At the hospital, he creates line-of-business applications for clinical, financial, and performance improvement.

Predominantly using Microsoft frameworks, Travis creates solutions that employ a wide range of technologies such as web, mobile, touch, and voice. Travis is a certified ASP.NET developer and has a Bachelor's degree in Business Administration emphasizing in Information Systems. He's currently enrolled in the Master's program at DePaul University's College of Digital Media. The focus of his study is Human–Computer Interaction and User-Centered Design.

Travis is the co-host of The Windows Developer Show (*http://www.windowsdeveloper show.com*), a weekly Internet broadcast for Microsoft developers, designers, and enthusiasts. In his off time (which doesn't exist), Travis enjoys reading, playing guitar, drawing, listening to music, and spending time with his family and friends.

To find out more about Travis, please visit *http://www.travislowdermilk.com* or follow him on Twitter (@tlowdermilk).

Colophon

The animal on the cover of *User-Centered Design* is a Spotted Nothura (*Nothura maculosa*), a species of bird called a tinamou, which is native to grassy habitats in eastern and southern Brazil, Paraguay, Uruguay, and northern Argentina. The Spotted Nothura is about 9 to 10 inches in length and patterned with brown and black mottling on a pale brownish base color. This provides good camouflage in its terrestrial grassland environment.

This species reproduces rapidly, as the female is mature within 2 months and can have five to six broods per year. The male will incubate the eggs and raise the chicks. Like most tinamous, the eggs have a spectacular glossy porcelain-like shell, which are colored a rich maroon or chocolate brown. The eggs are also considered of high nutritional value. While these birds eat seeds, including crops such as rice and soy, they also feed on insects and can be found near cattle where they eat both insects disturbed by the cattle and ticks feeding on the larger animals.

The cover image is from *Riverside Natural History*. The cover font is Adobe ITC Garamond. The text font is Adobe Minion Pro; the heading font is Adobe Myriad Condensed; and the code font is Dalton Maag's Ubuntu Mono.

Get even more for your money.

Join the O'Reilly Community, and register the O'Reilly books you own. It's free, and you'll get:

- $4.99 ebook upgrade offer
- 40% upgrade offer on O'Reilly print books
- Membership discounts on books and events
- Free lifetime updates to ebooks and videos
- Multiple ebook formats, DRM FREE
- Participation in the O'Reilly community
- Newsletters
- Account management
- 100% Satisfaction Guarantee

Signing up is easy:

1. **Go to: oreilly.com/go/register**
2. **Create an O'Reilly login.**
3. **Provide your address.**
4. **Register your books.**

Note: English-language books only

To order books online:
oreilly.com/store

For questions about products or an order:
orders@oreilly.com

To sign up to get topic-specific email announcements and/or news about upcoming books, conferences, special offers, and new technologies:
elists@oreilly.com

For technical questions about book content:
booktech@oreilly.com

To submit new book proposals to our editors:
proposals@oreilly.com

O'Reilly books are available in multiple DRM-free ebook formats. For more information:
oreilly.com/ebooks

O'REILLY®

Spreading the knowledge of innovators   oreilly.com